"For the sake of the comp[ ]
and planet, Tom Peters w[ ]
to—finally—put people first. He prods, provokes,
cajoles, and charms his way through catchy examples
and practical action steps that offer a path to
sustainable excellence."

—Rosabeth Moss Kanter, Harvard Business School professor, Author of *Think Outside the Building*

"Although Tom Peters writes with a sense of urgency,
savor his insights about what it takes to nurture our
companies—in his words, 'full-fledged breathing
communities,' and ensure business plays the role it
must in building the world we all deserve."

—Linda A. Hill, Wallace Brett Donham Professor of Business Administration, Harvard Business School; Faculty Chair, Leadership Initiative; Author of *Collective Genius: The Art and Practice of Leading Innovation*

"Tom's brilliant OPUS should not only be read and
reread but tucked under your pillow at night, so these
ideas seep in and guide our every behavior throughout
our lives."

—Jeanne Bliss, Bestselling Author and Customer Experience Expert

"If you don't have people as your true north before you
read *Excellence Now: Extreme Humanism*—you will at
the end. Tom gives us a master class in the 'soft stuff' –
what really matters today."

—Tiffani Bova, Growth Evangelist, Salesforce; WSJ Bestselling Author: *Growth IQ; Thinkers50*

"Tom Peters is the Gandalf of business. Human potential
is infinite magic, but most organizations blindly pursue
mindless mechanical contributions. Teams change the
world, leaders serve teams—and there's no such thing
as over-serving! If you want the secret of the quest,
Excellence Now: Extreme Humanism is a must read and
a must often reread."

—Linda Holliday, CEO and Founder of Citia

Excellence Now:

The Leadership 7/COVID-19

Be Kind.
Be Caring.
Be Patient.
Be Forgiving.
Be Positive.
Be Present.
Walk in the Other Person's Shoes.

Excellence Now:
Extreme Humanism

by Tom Peters

Print: 978-1-944027-94-0
eBook: 978-1-944027-93-3

un/teaching

www.networlding.com

Permissions
Grateful acknowledgement is made at the following link for
permission to reprint previously published material:
TomPeters.com/writing/books/excellence-now-extreme-
humanism/permissions

Designed by Donovan/Green.

Dedication

Robbin Reynolds, who by happenstance read an article of mine that appeared in *Business Week*, in July 1980, sent me unbidden a letter with a Harper & Row book contract attached, and commanded, "There's a book in that article." Hence, with a few steps in between, *In Search of Excellence*.

Nancy Austin, business partner and colleague, who said *In Search of Excellence* was missing action items and needed more energy; and thus became my inspiring co-author of *A Passion for Excellence*—and the primary source of my extreme use of italics, bold typeface, and, above all, Red Exclamation Marks!

Heather Shea, former president of my training company, The Tom Peters Company, who informed me one afternoon over a glass of chardonnay that I knew nothing about the puny representation and underutilized potential of women in leadership roles in business. She then convened a meeting of (very) powerful women and ordered me to be there; whence those women at Heather's command lectured me nonstop for three intense hours on my deficiencies—thereby launching my 25-year (1996-2021) obsession with women's market power and demonstrated leadership excellence.

Sally Helgesen, whose book *The Female Advantage* was my number one tutorial on women's issues in business. It, and Sally's subsequent work and good counsel, re-engineered many of my neural pathways—my life has never been the same.

Susan Cain. Seldom does a single book flip one's life upside down. Ms. Cain's 2013 book, *Quiet: The Power of Introverts in a World That Can't Stop Talking*, did just that. It is my easy pick as most impactful new business book of the century to date. Susan told me, personally and pointedly, or so it felt, that I was a hotshot "business guru" / "thought leader" who had effectively ignored half the working population, those introverts, whose contributions as leaders, for example, typically outshine the noisy buggers. Head bowed, I am forever in her debt.

Marianne Lewis, Dean of the Lindner College of Business at the University of Cincinnati. Dr. Lewis is using her tenure to re-invent business school education (so desperately in need of wholesale re-invention), putting the horribly misnamed "soft stuff" first— leadership, people, community, moral behavior, and excellence.

Susan Sargent, tapestry artist, home accessories designer-business owner whose approach to color changed an entire industry; and community organizer extraordinaire (conservation, climate change, the arts). Whose energy level makes the Energizer Bunny a snail by comparison—and my wife, colleague, and best friend for more than a quarter of a century.

Julie Anixter, Nancye Green, Melissa Wilson, and Shelley Dolley, for their tireless efforts to make this book, my "summa," the best it can possibly be—that is, excellent! Their professional contributions were exceptional and then some; at least as important, they became full partners and collaborators in this effort.

———————————

Note: This is not a dedication to "the women in my life." This is a dedication to eleven of the extraordinary professional women who have shaped my views about effective, diverse, humane, and morally-focused enterprises.

Foreword
by Vala Afshar

How can you focus on "excellence" after living through 2020, a year which brought the worst healthcare, economic, climate, racial and equality injustice, and large-scale dissemination of misinformation crises in a lifetime? Tom Peters' answer is to actively engage and to serve our employees, our communities, and the planet, to aim for no less than the betterment of society. And do it "with all your heart and all your soul and all your energy."

When business leaders' conversations turn to "excellence," they most often think of Tom Peters and *In Search of Excellence*, a book I first read in graduate school, which is widely considered to be one of the most influential management books of all time. Over the last 40+ years since that book, Tom has traveled to 50 states and 63 countries, presenting to over five million people. And now comes his 19th and, according to him, last book, *Excellence Now: Extreme Humanism*.

It is a book for today. Tom may have been around for quite a while, but there is no grass growing under his feet. He has taken to the digital age with a vengeance. His abundant daily engagements on Twitter are an example of constant excellence in advocacy for living and leading a commendable life. He has tweeted more than 125,000 times and earned over 170,000 followers. He is the principal reason I fell in love with Twitter. I first corresponded with Peters on Twitter, and he instantly became my mentor from afar. He is radically transparent and generous, willing to engage with everyone. The wisdom of Tom Peters, especially evident on

Twitter, is knowing that everyone you meet knows more than you about something.

Adhering to core values is my North Star as a leader. But my never-ending struggle is how to move from defining my values to delivering on my values, day in and day out. And how to inspire my colleagues to do the same. Where could I turn for guidance? Who could I trust? Was I alone on this journey? Amid asking for answers, I discovered Tom Peters, who would change my life personally and professionally. His message about the lifelong pursuit of excellence and moral behavior quieted the noise around me and helped me to know I wasn't alone. And you aren't either. That's why Tom wrote this book.

The first time I met Tom Peters in person was when he visited our Salesforce Boston office for a video interview. I greeted him in our lobby, expecting to see Peters and his entourage. He was alone, wearing a backpack and a sweater that I'd seen when watching his extensive library of leadership videos. He surprised me by pulling from his backpack my book, *The Pursuit of Social Business Excellence*. He has a wonderful way of showing appreciation and making people feel better about themselves.

In final preparation for our live interview, I saw Tom reviewing a thick folder of material covering a diverse set of topics including the importance of emotional intelligence, the benefits of promoting more women leaders, and the impact of artificial intelligence on the future of work. His excellent preparation led to a brilliant exchange. I have interviewed over 900 business leaders since 2013. The two that were most watched, approaching 300,000 views, are the pair of discussions with Tom Peters. What was even more remarkable was that Tom spent over two hours after our formal interview meeting with my colleagues, signing books, listening with interest, and answering hundreds of questions; then he quietly said goodbye and left. He inspired a dozen senior executives with humility, grace, and a spirit of generosity that was truly uplifting.

Why is *Excellence Now: Extreme Humanism* arguably Peters' most important contribution in his illustrious career? Forcefully, Tom says, "What you are doing right now will be the hallmark of your entire career." There are no truer words. In his book, Tom powerfully articulates how excellence in leadership is achieved by singularly focusing on helping others grow. Peters has long and passionately said that the job of a leader is not to gain more followers, but rather to develop more leaders.

Excellence Now is a must read for college students wanting to learn about how to succeed in business, for small business owners who deeply care about their employees and customers and communities, for middle managers, the most strategically important people in any businesses, and senior executives like me (in my case, working at the most successful and fastest growing technology company in the world), who understand the critical need to cultivate and maintain a culture of trust, personal growth, innovation, and true equality.

Excellence Now: Extreme Humanism is a beautiful reminder of what matters most as you pursue life and career goals. Putting people first by deeply and passionately caring about and abetting their holistic development and success; creating uplifting products and services that bring no less than joy into our lives; paying unstinting attention to details, knowing that small and continuous incremental improvements can add up to game-changing moments; recognizing the power of emotional intelligence and that the soft skills are the hardest skills to develop and the most important skills over the long haul. Peters also reminds us to have an unmistakable sense of urgency about big issues like the pressing need to for gender equality, the impact of climate change, and affordable and accessible education.

How long are you willing to wait to become the excellent leader you aspire to be? Communities, companies, and countries are in search of excellence now more than ever before as they wrestle with monumental dislocations of every sort. The question is whether you are the leader who will rise to the occasion and answer the call, who will commit to lead with integrity and humane values, regardless of the surrounding chaos and pressure.

Your true legacy is what people say about you when you are not in the room. How will you be remembered? Will you be described as kind, caring, patient, forgiving, present, and positive? In *Excellence Now*, Peters teaches us about the leadership characteristics that matter most at difficult times.

One of the most profound lessons I learned from Tom is that excellence, as he sees it, is not a long-term plan, not a mountain to climb. Excellence is the next conversation, the next meeting, or the next presentation. "Excellence is the next five minutes," says Peters, "or it is nothing at all."

I believe *Excellence Now: Extreme Humanism* is Tom Peters' best work, a culmination of four decades of data-driven research, collaborating with some of the most accomplished business and management leaders around the globe. I for one, plan to follow in his footsteps and learn as much as I can from a trailblazer like no other in the field of humanities, leadership, business, excellence, and life.

Vala Afshar, Chief Digital Evangelist, Salesforce
Author of *The Pursuit of Social Business Excellence*
Co-founder and co-host of the weekly podcast DisrupTV

Epigraphs

"Business exists to enhance human well-being."

—Mihaly Csikszentmihalyi, *Good Business*

"If you want something said, ask a man; if you want something done, ask a woman."

—Margaret Thatcher

"Creating excellence is not a job. Creating excellence is a moral act."

—Hugh MacLeod, gapingvoid

People and Community First

Products and Services That Serve Humanity

The Moral Responsibility of Enterprise

Now Far More Than Ever

Serendipity—perhaps a word used too often, but, in a strange way, the correct word in this instance.

- **March 2019:** Start work on my final book, summarizing forty-plus years of searching for excellence. Aim to make one last noisy plea for people and community first.

- **February 2020:** More or less complete draft goes to colleagues for comments.

- **March 2020:** COVID-19 shuts down the US and much of the world. Accompanying the pandemic earthquake, unemployment rolls in the U.S. alone increase by many millions.

- **June 2020:** Civil unrest sweeps the country. Protests over longstanding racial, political, and economic injustice and inequity portend a long and loud and extraordinarily important and overdue struggle.

- **Autumn 2020:** Most rancorous U.S. Presidential election in more than half a century—ever deeper fractures in society surface, with inequality at the head of the parade (wake?); no abatement in sight.

- **Autumn-Winter 2020-2021:** COVID-19 continues and—to use an overused term I dislike but that in this instance is apt—tumult settles in as the "new normal."

As to that serendipity, the multidimensional upheavals, piled on top of the AI job-destruction tsunami-in-progress and accelerating, makes this book's message far more timely, far more powerful, far more pertinent, and far more urgent than I could have imagined.

Leading amidst chaos. Leading amidst the personal and economic anguish brought on by COVID-19. Leading amidst the social pain symbolized by loud, angry, renewed awareness of immense racial inequities. Leading amidst political rancor that threatens the very roots of our democracy. Leading amidst an unmistakable truth that the staggering impact of climate change is not "coming"—it has arrived. How do leaders cope—and perhaps even thrive—as they move forward their efforts to serve their team members, the communities in which they are embedded, and the planet itself amidst this madness?

I reiterate for the umpteenth time, but with more urgency than ever before:

- People's engagement and growth *really* first.
- Community engagement *really* first.
- Planet Earth *really* first.
- Products and services that are not lookalikes-but-a-little-bit-cheaper, but that serve humanity and engender pride in our craft.
- Leaders who put creating and maintaining a caring and spirited and equitable culture *really* first.
- Now.

With *all* your heart and *all* your soul *and* all your energy.
No screwing around! Damn it!

It's head-shakingly bizarre to me, but I have been asked hundreds of times by so-called hard-nosed businesspeople: "Tom, why do you focus so damn much on this (soft) people stuff?" My best answer, other than what the hell else is there: people are exactly as important to a car dealer or a six- or 60 person accountancy—or Google—as they are to a football team or a symphony orchestra or the United States Marine Corps. That is, I repeat, people people people—yup, what the hell else is there?

An organization is not a sterilized org chart, a stack of job descriptions, and a zillion bloodless "efficiency first" processes. An organization is a full-fledged living, breathing *community* unto itself. An organization is a community embedded in communities—the hearths and homes of its employees, its customers, and its vendors' workers, too.

Our response to a crisis—this crisis, any crisis—will be the manifestation of how much and how consistently we care for others. The way I see it, from a leader's perspective, extreme care first and foremost emanates from unabashedly putting our people and our communities first.

I hope these pages will inspire you to action, in fact, extreme action. It's simple, really: extreme times call for no less than extreme responses. I even dare to hope that the new organizational cultures we might build in the face of today's madness will in fact usher in a widespread revolution marked by more humane and more energized workplaces committed to extreme (there's that word again) employee growth and the creation of products and services that are marked by excellence and even, dare I say it, make the world a wee bit better.

In closing: since this to me is, or will be received as, a so-called "business book," I would remind you that the data unequivocally say that "people first"—concern for long-term organizational and community health and producing products and services that matter—is far and away the most effective bottom-line business practice there is.

A Forty-Three-Year Journey of Hope

**This book is a "summa."
It is a "last hurrah."
It is an "I've done my
damnedest."
Please get cracking, with
extreme urgency.**

I have been chasing excellence for 43 years—since 1977, when the research for what became *In Search of Excellence* began. The work was ignited courtesy of my boss of bosses, the managing director of McKinsey & Company, where I was employed as a garden-variety consultant in our San Francisco office. The MD wondered why his talented consultants dreamed up ingenious, surefire business strategies, but clients found them difficult or impossible to implement. I had a dripping wet PhD from the Stanford Graduate School of Business; implementation was my dissertation topic—in fact, it was said to be the first of its kind and won several awards. I was given an unlimited budget to travel the world—literally—

in search of ideas about and examples of effective strategy implementation in big companies.

At one point, a year into the exercise, I was asked to make a client presentation on my assigned topic. The command was given by my big boss in San Francisco with less than twenty-four hours' notice. The night before the public declaiming I attended an extraordinary performance by the San Francisco Ballet. As I sat down to work upon returning from the ballet, and began to compose my remarks, an odd thought went through my mind.

Almost all adults work. We keep our jobs by serving our workmates, clients, customers, and communities effectively. Why couldn't that work—and that service to others—mimic the San Francisco Ballet? Why couldn't ballet excellence mark *our* business organizations of six or 600 and the work of those of us who ply our trade therein? I was so taken with the idea that I titled my short presentation the next day with a single word: *Excellence.* Though the reception to my presentation was positive, I was hardly off to the races. But the idea—this why-not-excellence-in-business thing—did stick, and I elaborated a bit and tried it on my widely dispersed team. And over time, my peers and then, especially and to my delight, our clients, took to the notion—and we *were* off to the races.

That was 43 years ago. And I have essentially not changed my tune in all those 43 years. I have spent, effectively, my adult life searching for individual and organizational excellence. My first book, co-written with Bob Waterman—a close pal all these years later—took off for a number of reasons, perfect timing not least among them. (The U.S. was beset by business malaise and a great recession.) Its impact was such that it became the most widely held book in American libraries from

1989 to 2006. Obviously, in retrospect, this "business-as-a-balletic performance" / "excellence-in-business" notion struck a chord.

I got—and get—lovely feedback, but have been enormously frustrated by the lack of an "excellence revolution." While any number have bought in—especially in small- and medium-sized enterprises—un-balletic enterprise performance has remained the norm. So, I've hunkered down and written seventeen more books and given more than 2,500 speeches in 63 countries since then. The books are by choice highly repetitive and do not require an understanding of rocket science to grasp:

- Take care of people—train them and train them and treat them with kindness and respect and help them prepare for tomorrow. Insist that every employee commit to encouraging growth and caring for their mates. This goes double—or triple—in today's troubled times. The goal is Extreme Employee Engagement (E-cubed). The bottom line is to make excellence the norm in all people matters. (The "bottom line" is also that this is the best way to grow and the best spur to profitability.)

- Make uplifting—a word chosen with great care—products and services that inspire our customers and make us smile and be proud of our efforts and maybe even make the world a tiny bit better. This is the bedrock of what I call Extreme Humanism. And this commandment holds for every industry and, yes, every internal department within the organization. (FYI: Products and services that exhibit "extreme humanism" and are "uplifting" are also the best defense against the AI tsunami.)

- "Small > big" is my mantra—a blizzard of small steps and memorable touches are more important than "breakthrough" attempts. So, take those constant small steps forward into the unknown—"serious play" as one guru puts it—hour after hour after hour, day after day after day. Every single one of us—100 percent of us!—can be and must be an innovator!

- Embrace the urgency required to deal with—in your sphere of influence—the catastrophic implications of climate change. The time for half measures is past. Climate change implications are not "around the corner." They have arrived.

- Behave honorably at all times and be an excellent and vigorous community member and moral leader. Be able to describe your work and service activities to family members with pride, maybe even delight.

- Aim for excellence day in and day out, not as a grand aspiration, but as a way of life that is even expressed or not in, yes, your next 10 line email.

These notions add up to you and me and our peers doing work of value, work that engenders pride in every stakeholder—and, as previously noted, this flavor of work pays off to a startling degree in terms of the standard business measures of sustained growth and top-tier profitability.

There are 75 ideas with accompanying "To-Dos" presented in this book. Implemented with determination and verve and 100 percent participation, they are, to go out on a limb and express my faith in you, guaranteed to work and have been demonstrated to work time and time again under circumstances of every conceivable flavor.

The Hour of Reckoning Is Upon Us

We are in the grip of COVID-19 and the most significant social and political unrest in the U.S. since the mid-1960s—what can only be called once-in-a-lifetime chaos. We have—in the business world and beyond—seen organizations and leaders react well, with compassion and care. And we have seen other organizations and their leaders stick to traditional efficiency-and-output-maximization dogma and at times behave in callous, even reprehensible, ways.

Insane as things are, excellence as portrayed in this book is, to my mind, far *more* important and urgent than ever. Excellence is an encompassing and a 24 / 7 / 60 / 60 activity. It is a must. There is no moral "dimension" to excellence. Excellence as defined here *is* the whole ballgame and must be reflected in every step we (every one of us) take. Humane and thoughtful and caring and inclusive gestures toward our team members, our communities, and our customers must become our bread and butter and meat and potatoes. They are not "part of us." They *are* us. Yes, damn it, we must stop futzing around on issues such as race and gender—and make addressing these issues a, or even *the*, centerpiece of our organizational mission and strategy and daily action assessments. And maybe, just maybe, when the worst of today's turbulence has passed, we can usher in a new era where *people first* and *caring and compassionate* and *inclusive leadership* and *excellence in all we do* become the norm—rather than provenance of all too few.

Leadership Seven / COVID-19

Be kind.
Be caring.
Be patient.
Be forgiving.
Be present.
Be positive.

Walk in the other person's shoes.
In short: this is an unparalleled opportunity to enact positive change and plant the seeds for a better world. To react with less than full-scale engagement and commitment is, to me, unconscionable. Please act. Don't blow it!

Excellence. Now.
People First. Now.
Extreme Humanism. Now.
Your Legacy. Now. (Or Not.)

What's contained in these pages, I believe, is a reasonably complete roadmap to a world of excellence, extreme humanism, people first, caring and compassionate and inclusive enterprise leadership. To follow the roadmap will not make our current COVID-19, social, and political troubles disappear. It can, however, lead to the creation or maintenance of an organization "desperately" committed to the growth of all its members and the wellbeing of the communities in which it operates. That is a contribution that every leader can work toward every day—and it *is* a contribution to addressing, in some small way, the extraordinary issues that confront us all.

How wonderful and uplifting the achievement of these aims would be for our team members, our customers, our communities, and for us as individuals. But the success will be no cake walk.

The journey begins today. In blunt terms: how you, as leaders (the modal reader of this book is a leader—well, actually, we should and can *all* be leaders), behave—*right now in the midst of crisis*—will likely be a, or *the*, principal determinant of your life legacy. For better or for worse.

People first / Extreme Employee Engagement.
(Or not.)
Now.
(Or never.)

Caring and compassionate and inclusive leadership.
(Or not.)
Now.
(Or never.)

Extreme Community Engagement.
(Or not.)
Now.
(Or never.)

Extreme Sustainability.
(Or not.)
Now.
(Or never.)

Products and services that inspire, that make the world just a little bit better, and that make us proud.
(Or not.)
Now.
(Or never.)

Extreme Humanism in all we do.
(Or not.)
Now.
(Or never.)

Excellence in all we do.
(Or not.)
Now.
(Or never.)

"Resume Virtues" vs. "Eulogy Virtues"

"I've been thinking about the difference between the 'resume virtues' and the 'eulogy virtues.' The resume virtues are the ones you list on your resume, the skills that you bring to the job market and that contribute to external success. The eulogy virtues are deeper. They're the virtues that get talked about at your funeral, the ones that exist at the core of your being—whether you are kind, brave, honest or faithful, what kind of relationships you formed."
—David Brooks, *The Road to Character*

On the Shoulders of Giants

I am, needless to say, delighted when people say kind things about my work. But the fact is, to not coin a phrase, I ride on the shoulders of giants. A 50 slide PowerPoint presentation I use for a speech will include thirty or so quotes by a sterling cast of others.

Hence, in this book, I am letting the shoulders of those others—the likes of Southwest Airlines' Herb Kelleher and Colleen Barrett, Margaret Thatcher, the inimitable Sir Richard Branson, Advertising Hall of Fame and entrepreneurial star Linda Kaplan Thaler, and even Ben Franklin—carry the lion's share of the load. Their words, not mine, will almost always come first. I will simply be the organizer and succinct commentator and your persistent nudger-in-chief. After all, they, those giants, not I, are the "real people" who have committed to excellence and created amazing enterprises staffed by fully engaged and extraordinarily well-trained people consistently delivering memorable, emotionally engaging, spiritually uplifting products and services to their customers (a mouthful, but largely an accurate assessment). So pay attention to them. And learn from *them*.

A Plea

By my standards, this is a rather slim book—my *Liberation Management* was 900 pages long. And as I implied above, the book is in effect a library of about 300 quotes, culled from the thousands upon thousands that sit in my PowerPoint library. Well, the truth of the matter is that you could make it through those quotes, probably nodding your head often as not, in an hour—or two or three hours at the most..

But here is my grand request, my plea. You could, yes, "make it through" the set of quotes in a flash. However, my fond hope is that it will take you months, or years, or the eternity of your professional career to really (really) make it through this basketful of observations or prescriptions. As I imagine it (or hope), you will chew on these Bransonisms or Kelleherisms, toss them around in your head, then chew a bit more, discuss some of the most profound observations with friends and colleagues. It's fair to say that virtually every one of these quotes captures and spells out a way of life.

For example, ponder this from Richard Sheridan, CEO of the successful software firm Menlo Innovations: *"It may sound radical, unconventional, and bordering on being a crazy business idea. However—as ridiculous as it sounds—joy is the core belief of our workplace. Joy is the reason my company exists. It is the single shared belief of our entire team."*

Now *there* is an "out of the box" idea! Ye gads, "joy is the reason my company exists." And he means it and lives it, and the results show it. Though extreme, could *you* imagine this phenomenon in your world? A hasty answer would be an insult to Mr. Sheridan—and me.

I will give you no less than a guarantee. These words, as I said, came from the mouths or pens or keyboards of incredibly thoughtful people. These quotes are their summaries, or coda, of lives well lived, contributions that have made the world a bit better in every setting imaginable.

So instead of a look-and-nod-and-on-to-the-next-one, reflect and reflect and reflect some more. "Hmmmmm, could that be applied in *my* world???"

Yes:
Reflect!
Reflect!
Reflect!
And act, alone or in concert with your peers, on the ones that make sense.

Please! Damn It!

Look, I care about this stuff. I care about it enough to have traveled to 63 countries and logged about over 3,000,000 miles and god alone knows how many "red eyes" trying to tell this story. To beg my audiences to take the likes of Richard Sheridan (see above) seriously. I really really care about "all this," and, damn it, I know it works.

I am 78. This is my last gasp—my final Big Effort to get through to leaders and non-leaders in businesses and non-businesses.

Please.
Please.
(Damn it!)

Table of Contents

15 Topics & 75 To Dos

Using this book:

There are no chapters. Instead, there are 15 topics and 75 "To Dos". The Table of Contents will display the topic number / title in bold and the "To Dos" will be numbered underneath.

Throughout this book, there are specific, actionable, "To Do's" highlighted by a grey box.

Topic *To Do*

1.2

Hiring:
Soft Skills, EQ First,
100 Percent of Jobs

"In short, hiring is the most important aspect of business and yet remains woefully misunderstood."
—Philip Delves Broughton, "The Hard Work of Getting Ahead," *Wall Street Journal*

To Do: 2A Dear boss, can you honestly declare that you are a full-fledged *hiring professional*? And if not, what are you going to do about it? This is *your* damned job—the most important aspect of business. It is not to be left to the people department folks.

"The ultimate filter we use [in the hiring process] is that we only hire nice people. When we finish assessing skills, we do something called 'running the gauntlet.' We have them interact with 15 or 20 people, and every one of them has what I call a 'blackball vote,' which means they can say if we should not hire that person. I believe in culture so strongly and that one bad apple can spoil the bunch. There are enough really talented people out there who are nice—you don't really need to put up with people who act like jerks."
—Peter Miller, CEO, Optinose

To Dos

3 "Strategy Is a Commodity. Execution Is an Art."

Page 86

4 People *Really* First. "Business Has to Give People Enriching, Rewarding Lives . . . or It's Simply Not Worth Doing."

Page 94

8 Value-Added Strategy #3: Top-Line Focus

Page 158

8.36 Value-Added Strategy #3: Better Before Cheaper, Revenue Before Cost, There Are No Other Rules

9 Value-Added Strategy #4: There Need Be No Such Thing as a Commodity, Garage as Cultural Icon, Plumber as Artist

Page 162

9.37 Value-Added Strategy #4: There Need Be No Such Thing as a Commodity, Garage as Cultural Icon, Plumber as Artist

10 Value-Added Strategy #5: Services Added. "We'll Do Anything and Everything for You."

Page 168

10.38 Value-Added Strategy #5: Services (of Every Conceivable Flavor) Added. "We'll Do Anything and Everything for You." Department as "Cost- Center" to Department as Value-Added "Superstar Professional Service Firm"

11
Value-Added Strategy #6: Page 174
A Bold Social Media Strategy, The "20-5" Rule, One Tweet > A Super Bowl Ad, You *Are* Your Social Media Strategy

12
Value-Added Strategies Page 178
#7 & #8:
Women Buy *Everything*. "Oldies" Have *All* the Money.

13

WTTMSW / Whoever Tries The Most Stuff (And Screws The Most Stuff Up The Fastest) Wins. Serious Play is the Essence of Innovation. Fail. Forward. Fast. Diversity Trumps Ability. Learn Not to be Careful.

14

Leading with Compassion and Care, Twenty-One Proven Tactics

15 Executive Summary

15.75   Excellence Now: The Forty-Three Number Ones

1

First Things Before
First Things

1.1

Hard (Numbers / Plans / Org Charts) Is Soft.

Soft (People / Relationships / Culture) Is Hard.

"The terms 'hard facts' and 'the soft stuff' used in business imply that data are somehow real and strong while emotions are weak and less important."

—George Kohlrieser, *Hostage at the Table: How Leaders Can Overcome Conflict, Influence Others, and Raise Performance*

My life in six words: Hard is soft. Soft is hard.

Hard (numbers / plans / org charts) is soft: Plans are often fantasies; organizational charts have little to do with the way the organization actually works; and numbers are readily manipulated. Case in point: "quants" and ratings-agency staffers cleverly packaged and evaluated "derivatives" of valueless mortgages, thus spurring the multitrillion-dollar financial crash of 2007–2008 and beyond.

Soft (people / relationships / culture) is hard: The best "people practices" (caring, training, acknowledging) create the most wholesome, community-minded organizations—and win in the marketplace as well. Effective people practices, design that inspires, customers who are enthralled, vendors who bend over backwards to assist us are all byproducts of a supportive culture nurtured one day at a time.

This was the heart of *In Search of Excellence*. This is the heart of my work today. This has been the heart of every one of my books. "Hard is soft / soft is hard" has been taken up by some, but I'm afraid it's not the norm. And as I write, we are in the grip of COVID-19 and deep social and political unrest. Humane and thoughtful behavior is in fact more important than ever. Far more important!

To Do: **1A**	Hard is soft. Soft is hard. The time has come. The time is now. Put first things first, starting with your next face-to-face or WFH / work from home / Zoom meeting.

Google's Big, Soft Surprises

"Project Oxygen shocked everyone by concluding that, among the eight most important qualities of Google's top employees, STEM expertise comes in dead last. The seven top characteristics of success at Google are all soft skills: being a good coach; communicating and listening well; possessing insights into others (including others' different values and points of view); having empathy toward and being supportive of one's colleagues; being a good critical thinker and problem solver; and being able to make connections across complex ideas. Those traits sound more like what one gets as an English or theater major than as a programmer.

"Project Aristotle . . . further supports the importance of soft skills even in high-tech environments. Project Aristotle analyzes data on inventive and productive teams. Google takes pride in its A-teams, assembled with top scientists, each with the most specialized knowledge and able to throw down one cutting-edge idea after another. Its data analysis revealed, however, that the company's most important and productive ideas come from B-teams comprised of employees that don't always have to be the smartest people in the room. Project Aristotle shows that the best teams at Google exhibit a range of soft skills: equality, generosity, curiosity toward the ideas of your teammates, empathy, and emotional intelligence. And topping the list: emotional safety. No bullying."

—Valerie Strauss, "The Surprising Thing Google Learned About Its Employees—and What It Means for Today's Students," *Washington Post*

"Soft stuff" is at least as important in super high-tech Google / Silicon Valley as it is for the table-staff at a restaurant in Annapolis, Maryland. This is a dynamite revelation, which did not in the least, in retrospect, surprise me. It should also be a clarion call to action for *every* leader.

To Do: 1B I, an old pro who has "seen it all," did a double take—triple take?—when I read the Google report. Maybe there was even a gasp. I dearly hope you gasp. And then read slowly three or four times. And share widely. And discuss intensely. (You should be able to create a truckload of your own To Dos from this. Could the message be any more clear? And, again, from *Google*, for heaven's sake.)

Soft Is Hard: "Compassionomics"

Compassion Saves Lives

Compassion Boosts the Bottom Line

"We are often led to believe that sentiments like compassion and kindness are expressions of weakness rather than signs of strength. And we are often all too ready to give into the false belief that meanness somehow equates to toughness and that empathy is empty of power. But the evidence in this book suggests the opposite."

--from the foreword, by Senator Cory Booker, to the book *Compassionomics*

Compassionomics: The Revolutionary Scientific Evidence That Caring Makes a Difference is a book by two healthcare researchers-practitioners. It is a healthcare book. Except it is not. It is a leadership book—the best one I've read in years. It is a business book—about behaviors that provide dramatically better results, regardless of the context in which those behaviors occur. And *Compassionomics* may provide the best illustration of "Hard is soft. Soft is hard." that I have come across.

The lead co-author, Stephen Trzeciak, is an MD and a researcher. He is not just a "researcher." He is a hardnosed, take-no-prisoners, quant researcher. And his and Dr. Mazzarelli's book is chock-a-block with reports on meticulously vetted quant research. But the topic is compassion. And the overwhelming evidence is that compassion pays in healthcare settings. Not only does it save innumerable lives (speed up healing, reduce side effects, improve mental acuity, and more), the most important outcomes, but it also routinely leads to dramatically better financial results for healthcare providers.

From the introduction: *"You might be surprised to learn that Darwin did not originate the phrase 'survival of the fittest,' for which he is known. It was actually Herbert Spencer, a noted British biologist and anthropologist, who coined the phrase after reading Darwin's views on evolution. Over time, this framing became misconstrued into the widely-held belief that Darwin's views were justification for aggressive, gladiator-like behavior.*

"What Darwin actually concluded was different and even more remarkable. According to Darwin, the communities with the greatest compassion for others would 'flourish the best and rear the greatest number of offspring.' In short, the body of scientific evidence supports that compassion actually protects the species."

Page after page, chapter after chapter, Doctors Trzeciak and Mazzarelli provide compelling and irrefutable evidence of the power of compassion. I say to my readers, unequivocally, that the research reported in *Compassionomics*—which, I repeat, is the best leadership book I have come across in years— applies one-for-one (make that 1.001 for 1.001) to any business or other organizational setting imaginable.

Read the book.
Share the book with others.
Act on the book's unassailable conclusions.
Compassion makes lives better.
Compassion saves lives.
Compassion pays.
Hard is soft. Soft is hard.

To Do:
1C
Do not in fact "read this book." Instead: Study this book. Translate it into your world. With your peers, create an action item list. (Keep in mind, that getting really serious about putting

your version of "compassionomics" to work requires going deep—and altering your organization culture.

The Soft Edge

"I believe the business world is at a crossroads, where hard-edge people are dominating the narrative and discussion. . . . The battle for money and attention boiling inside most companies and among most managers is that between the hard and soft edges. . . .

"Far too many companies invest too little time and money in their soft-edge excellence. . . . The three main reasons for this mistake are:

- *The hard edge is easier to quantify.*

- *Successful hard-edge investment provides a faster return on investment.*

- *CEOs, CFOs, chief operating officers, boards of directors, and shareholders speak the language of finance. . . .*

"Let me now make the case for investing time and money in your company's soft edge:

- *Soft-edge strength leads to greater brand recognition and higher profit margins; it is the ticket out of Commodityville.*

- *Companies strong in the soft edge are better prepared to survive a big strategic mistake or cataclysmic disruption . . .*

- *Hard-edge strength is absolutely necessary to compete, but it provides a fleeting advantage."*

—Rich Karlgaard, *The Soft Edge: Where Great Companies Find Lasting Success*

The Soft Edge: Where Great Companies Find Lasting Success, has section titles that support this message: "Trust." "Teams." "Taste." "Smarts." "Story."

Full disclosure: I like Rich Karlgaard's definition of "soft" better than my own! And I am no less than thrilled that he devoted an entire book to this subject—perhaps a first of its kind.

"Soft Stuff": Missing in Action

"When I was in medical school, I spent hundreds of hours looking into a microscope—a skill I never needed to know or ever use. Yet I didn't have a single class that taught me communication or teamwork skills, something I need every day I walk into the hospital."

—Peter Pronovost, *Safe Patients, Smart Hospitals: How One Doctor's Checklist Can Help Us Change Healthcare from the Inside Out*

Pronovost, who ran Johns Hopkins' ICU, brought checklists into healthcare—and has been responsible for saving tens of thousands of lives. Professional schools in general—for example, medicine, engineering, business—have a wretched track record when it comes to paying attention to the "soft stuff." Addressing that deficit of epic proportion is a, if not the, top life goal for me.

"As I sat there listening to one presentation after another highlighting the remarkable and unorthodox activities [people first dogma, leadership style, communal culture, etc.] that have made this organization so healthy, I leaned

over and quietly asked the CEO a rhetorical question,
'Why in the world don't your competitors do any of this?'
After a few seconds he whispered, almost sadly, 'You
know, I honestly believe they think it's beneath them.'"

—Patrick Lencioni, *The Advantage: Why Organizational Health Trumps Everything Else in Business*

To Do:
1D

"They think it is beneath them." Alas, my decades of observation lead me to think this is very true. Where are you on this? *No hasty answers. Please.* Reflect on your last meeting, the last week, the last significant conversation with one of your team members. Does it reflect and clearly signal primary attention to the "soft stuff?" I can do no more than beg you to put the soft stuff at the top of *your* agenda—permanently. And realize that, regardless of industry, *you are in the soft stuff business!*

Hard Is Soft / Soft Is Hard / Now Is The Hour (I Hope)

My last 43 years have indeed been "religiously" (almost the right word) pushing for / shouting for / begging for *Hard is soft. Soft is hard.* Alas, I have been less successful than I had hoped—by a long shot. But there is a chance, accelerated by the chaos that surrounds us, that the moment has come where those six words will take their place at the head of the line. (Even in MBA programs?)

Some leaders have behaved admirably in the face of the madness that has resulted from COVID-19 and explosive social unrest. Some have not.

Memories are long. And I believe that those who behaved well—those who put people truly first—may finally move center stage and nudge to the side the professional cost-cutters, mindless technology adopters, and soulless "shareholder value maximizers." The phrase "the new normal" has been horridly overused, but maybe, just maybe, this is the *Hard is soft. Soft is hard* moment. Leaders who buy in— in enterprises, from tiny to enormous, and particularly given the consequences of the pandemic and our greatly enhanced awareness of staggering social inequity—will become our premier and celebrated role models.

Hard Is Soft / Soft Is Hard / Last Words

"The first step is to measure what can easily be measured. This is okay as far as it goes.

"The second step is to disregard that which cannot be measured, or give it an arbitrary quantitative value. This is artificial and misleading.

"The third step is to presume that what cannot be measured is not very important. This is blindness.

"The fourth step is to say what cannot be measured does not really exist. This is suicide."

—Daniel Yankelovich, on the limitations of analytic models

1.2

Hiring:
Soft Skills, EQ First,
100 Percent of Jobs

*"In short, hiring is the most important aspect of business
and yet remains woefully misunderstood."*

—Philip Delves Broughton, "The Hard Work of Getting Ahead," *Wall Street Journal*

To Do:
2A

Dear boss, can you honestly declare that you are a full-fledged
hiring professional? And if not, what are you going to do about
it? This is *your* damned job—the most important aspect of
business. It is not to be left to the people department folks.

*"The ultimate filter we use [in the hiring process] is that
we only hire nice people. When we finish assessing
skills, we do something called 'running the gauntlet.' We
have them interact with 15 or 20 people, and every one
of them has what I call a 'blackball vote,' which means
they can say if we should not hire that person. I believe
in culture so strongly and that one bad apple can spoil
the bunch. There are enough really talented people out
there who are nice—you don't really need to put up with
people who act like jerks."*

—Peter Miller, CEO, Optinose

To Do: 2B Read. Reread. Share. Pharmaceuticals is not the sector in which you'd expect such words. Pay particular attention to "enough really talented people out there who are nice."

To Do: 2C Hire nice people. One hundred percent of jobs. If not, *why not*?

"When we talk about the qualities we want in people, empathy is a big one. If you can empathize with people, then you can do a good job. If you have no ability to empathize, . . . then it's difficult to help people improve. Everything becomes harder. One way that empathy manifests itself is courtesy. . . . It's not just about having a veneer of politeness, but actually trying to anticipate someone else's needs and meeting them in advance."

—Stewart Butterfield, co-founder and CEO of Slack

"We look for people that are warm and caring and actually altruistic. We look for people who have a fun-loving attitude."

—Colleen Barrett, former president, Southwest Airlines

"I can't tell you how many times we passed up hotshots for guys we thought were better people and watched our guys do a lot better than the big names, not just in the classroom, but on the field—and, naturally, after they graduated, too. Again and again, the blue chips faded out, and our little up-and-comers clawed their way to all-conference and All-American teams."

—Bo Schembechler, legendary football coach on character, *Bo's Lasting Lessons: The Legendary Coach Teaches the Timeless Fundamentals of Leadership*

Hiring For EQ:
1.7 Percent vs. 50–77 Percent

"What I thought nursing involved when I started: chemistry, biology, physics, pharmacology, and anatomy. And what I now know to be the truth of nursing: philosophy, psychology, art, ethics, and politics."

—Christie Watson, *The Language of Kindness: A Nurse's Story*

"We also draw from our experiences at the University of Pennsylvania's IMPaCT program, where we have developed an innovative approach to hiring community health workers [CHWs], a rapidly growing segment of the healthcare workforce. Our approach has resulted in a turnover rate of 1.7% compared with an industry standard of 50–77% per year. And indeed the people we've hired achieve results: multiple randomized controlled trials demonstrated that our CHWs have helped improve health and quality while reducing hospital days by 65%. . . .

"What helps people become and stay healthy? . . . We asked thousands of high-risk patients and made a list of barriers patients were facing. We brainstormed potential solutions, then listed the attributes that a worker would need. . . . Attributes like community membership and altruism rose to the top of our wish list . . . Just as important were the attributes that, surprisingly, were missing from our list—college and graduate degrees, or even previous clinical training. . . . Resumes, diplomas, and training certificates are commonly evaluated credentials healthcare organizations use to assess candidates. . . . They shed little light on personality traits or attitudes."

—Elena Butler and Shreya Kangovi, "Health Care Providers Are Hiring the Wrong People," *Harvard Business Review*

To Do:
2D
I wouldn't think this requires much explanation other than a repeat: 50–77 percent to 1.7 percent turnover. Sixty-five percent reduced hospitalization. Please reflect. Then translate into action. *Now.*

Hiring:
Plain Language Please!

Nice.

Empathy.

Courteous.

Listening.

Warm.

Caring.

Altruistic.

Smiling.

Saying "thank you."

Community membership.

Service orientation.

"Better people."

No jerks.

To Do:
2E
Are such attributes—*in the precise language used here, not the stilted bureaucratic version—formal* hiring requirements for *every* position in your organization? If not, *why not*?

Hiring "Soft" Redux:
Loving the Unloved Liberal Arts Degree

At graduation, business and professional degree holders in general (MBAs, engineers, lawyers, and so on) have higher interview and hire rates, and higher starting salaries, than new liberal arts grads.

By year 20, liberal arts grads have risen farther than their biz-professional degree holder peers. At one giant tech firm, 43 percent of liberal arts grads had made it to upper-middle management compared to 32 percent of engineering grads. At one giant financial services firm, 60 percent of the worst managers, according to company evaluations, had MBAs, while 60 percent of the best had only BAs.

—derived from research by Michael Useem, reported in Henry Mintzberg's *A Hard Look at the Soft Practice of Managing and Management Development*

Sample among these:

- *The Fuzzy and the Techie: Why the Liberal Arts Will Rule the Digital World,* by Scott Hartley
- *You Can Do Anything: The Surprising Power of a "Useless" Liberal Arts Education,* by George Anders
- *Sensemaking: The Power of the Humanities in the Age of the Algorithm,* by Christian Madsbjerg
- *Range: Why Generalists Triumph in a Specialized World,* by David Epstein

To Do:
2F
Regardless of the nature of the enterprise, seek out liberal arts job candidates. More theater majors! More philosophy majors! More history majors! Please!

1.3

Training: Enterprise Capital Investment #1

"training,
TRAINING,
and M-O-R-E
T-R-A-I-N-I-N-G

—Admiral Chester Nimitz, Commander in Chief / Pacific, communication to Chief of Naval Operations Ernest King in 1943. The U.S. Navy was woefully underprepared at the time of Pearl Harbor. The fix? Training. Training was more important than equipment, per Nimitz. (Note: Capitalization, punctuation, italics are Nimitz's, not mine.)

If you don't think training is of paramount importance, ask an Army general, a Navy admiral, an Air Force general, a football coach, an archery coach, a fire chief, a police chief, a theater director, a pilot, the head of an ER or ICU, the operations chief of a nuclear power plant, or a great restaurateur. Training is a *capital* expense—and no less than Enterprise Investment #1.

I remain staggered that in business, which occupies most of us, regular "fireman-like" training, growth, and development are rare. A course here and there, a meeting now and then, but not a constant professional preoccupation.

Let me be clear: This holds for a one-person or six-person company where each person is, by definition, central, as well as bigger outfits.

"Essentially, I was always more of a practice coach than a game coach. This is because of my conviction that a player who practices well, plays well."
—John Wooden, *They Call Me Coach*

"Everybody has a will to win. What's far more important is having the will to prepare to win."
—Bobby Knight, *Knight, My Story*

"Give me six hours to chop down a tree, and I will spend the first four sharpening the axe."
—Abraham Lincoln

I have given a jillion speeches, more or less on the same topic. Yet, preparing for my next 45-minute speech will take about 30 hours. *Preparing is what I do for a living—the rest, really, is details.*

The Training Queries:
If Not, Why Not?

Is your Chief Training Officer (CTO) your top paid C-level job, other than CEO / COO? If not, *why not*? Of course, I know you probably don't even *have* a Chief Training Officer. And your CTO is the Chief Technology Officer, right? For shame. And how stupid.

Are your top trainers paid as much as and treated as well as your top marketers or engineers? If not, *why not*?

Are your training courses so good-awesome-excellent that they make you tingle? If not, *why not*?

If you randomly stop an employee in the hall, can they describe in detail their training and development plan for the next 12 months? If not, *why not*?

My Big Four Dispiriting Bets:

Bet #1: > 5 of 10 CEOs see training as an expense rather than an investment.

Bet #2: > 5 of 10 CEOs see training as defense rather than offense.

Bet #3: > 5 of 10 CEOs see training as a necessary evil rather than a strategic opportunity.

Bet #4: > 8 of 10 CEOs, in a 45 minute tour d'horizon of their business, would not so much as mention training.

The sky-high likelihood of my winning all four of these bets is a mark of gross leader stupidity.

To Do: 3A   I have said unmistakably: training = Capital Investment #1, now more than ever—as we seek differentiation in the age of AI. Please chew—and chew and chew—on that. Do you agree? If not, *why not*?

To Do: 3B   Review in detail your approach to and investment in training. Thoroughly assess the quality of each of your training courses. Assess the quality of the training staff. Assess the level of training for each and every employee. This is a premier *strategic* issue; the effort should not be done in haste. (You may need the assistance of an outsider.)

Training: A Training and Learning Culture

Training on the scale I am suggesting is far more than a programmatic activity. I acknowledge that I will repeatedly say such a thing, but training-as-Capital Investment-#1 is a way of being, a premier cultural attribute. Topic Three, People First, describes an environment wholeheartedly devoted to Extreme Employee Engagement and growth. And at the tiptop of the list of extreme employee growth enhancers is . . . "training, TRAINING, and M-O-R-E T-R-A-I-N-I-N-G."

To Do: 3C Would you describe training and development as a premier cultural attribute in your organization? And do you agree it should be? Please discuss widely and brutally. (Be harsh on yourself, if appropriate).

Training: The Last Word

"Train people well enough so they can leave, treat them well enough so they don't want to."

—Richard Branson, in a Tweet

Training: The Last Harangue

Q: What is the difference in training needs between my local Subaru dealer, a nearby 25-table restaurant, the nine-person appliance repair business that helps us out, the San Francisco Symphony, and San Francisco 49ers?

A: There is no difference.

Got it?

1.4

Frontline Leaders Are Corporate Strength #1

"In great armies, the job of generals is to back up their sergeants."

—Colonel Tom Wilhelm, in Robert Kaplan's "The Man Who Would Be Khan," *Atlantic*

FACT: If the regimental commander lost most of his second lieutenants and first lieutenants and captains and majors, it would be a tragedy. If he lost his sergeants, it would be a catastrophe.

FACT: The Army and the Navy are fully aware that success on the battlefield is dependent to an overwhelming degree on its sergeants and chief petty officers—that is, its population of frontline managers.

Does industry have the same awareness as the military? My answer: No!

Do enterprises think that getting the right person to fill a frontline chief slot is important? Sure.

But do they view the full collection of frontline leaders as no less than Corporate Strength #1?
No!

Not "getting this" is a strategic mistake of the first order. See below.

Frontline Leaders

Frontline leaders are . . .

- Principal determinants of enterprise productivity
- Principal determinants of employee retention
- Principal determinants of product and service quality
- Principal carriers and embodiments of corporate culture
- Principal visible spear carriers for excellence
- Principal champions and enablers of sustained employee development
- Principal drivers of cross-functional excellence
- Enterprise Strength #1

An imposing list, eh? And not an iota of exaggeration. I simply ask you to reflect on the last: Enterprise Strength #1. It is closed-case-obvious if you buy into the list above. The frontline bosses are the principal determinants of damn near everything that's important. Hence, automatically, Enterprise Strength #1.

Seven Key Questions About Frontline Leaders:

1. Do you absolutely understand and act upon the fact that the frontline leader is the key leadership role in the organization?
2. Do the people professionals (and top management in general) single out frontline bosses individually and collectively for special developmental attention?
3. Do you spend gobs and gobs (and gobs) of time selecting frontline supervisors?

4. Are you willing, pain notwithstanding, to leave a frontline supervisor slot open until you can fill it with somebody spectacular?
5. Do you have the absolute best training and continuing development programs in the industry for frontline supervisors?
6. Do you formally and rigorously and continuously mentor frontline supervisors?
7. Are your frontline supervisors accorded the attention and acknowledgment and respect that their position merits?

To Do: 4A Carefully analyze the seven questions above. Where do you stand on each of these questions?

To Do: 4B Re-read this section with total attention before you fill your next open frontline leader slot.

Frontline Leaders: Bottom Line

Worldwide, with virtually no exception, some 50 to 75 percent of employees are "not engaged" in their work. One cause tops the list: bad bosses. Begin—immediately—a deep-dive assessment of your frontline chiefs. No strategic move could be more important than upgrading the quality of your full portfolio of frontline chiefs.

To Do: 4C Consider launching a formal 'Frontline Leaders Excellence Program.' Make it a first-order strategic priority. Right now.

1.5

Women Rule (or Should)

"If you want something said, ask a man; if you want something done, ask a woman."

—Margaret Thatcher, Speech to National Union of Townswomen's Guilds Conference

A Truckload of Evidence Says Women Are the Best Leaders

"Research [by McKinsey & Company] suggests that, in order to succeed, companies should start by promoting women."

—Nicholas Kristof, "Twitter, Women and Power," *New York Times*

"McKinsey & Company found that the international companies with more women on their corporate boards far outperformed the average company in return on equity and other measures. Operating profit was 56 percent higher."

—Nicholas Kristof, "Twitter, Women and Power," *New York Times*

"As leaders, women rule: New studies find that female managers outshine their male counterparts on almost every measure."

—Bloomberg BusinessWeek, Special Section title

"Women are rated higher in fully 12 of 16 competencies that go into outstanding leadership. And two of the traits where women outscored men to the highest degree— taking initiative and driving for results—have long been thought of as particularly male strengths."

—Jack Zenger and Joseph Folkman, "Are Women Better Leaders than Men?" *Harvard Business Review*

Throughout this section you will find "Women are (better leaders, etc)." I am obviously implying "on average." There are great male leaders and awful women leaders. But "on average"—and often to a significant degree!—women are better at this or that.

"In my experience, women make much better executives than men."

—Kip Tindell, CEO of the Container Store, *Uncontainable: How Passion, Commitment, and Conscious Capitalism Built a Business Where Everyone Thrives*

With this small batch of quotes, I am neither suggesting "case closed" (though I more or less think it is) nor that we toss all male leaders into the rubbish bin.

I am suggesting, in no uncertain terms, that if a leadership team does not have a significant share of women—certainly no less than 40 percent—your organization is making a first-order strategic performance error.

Alas, There Is a Long Way to Go

"Fewer large companies are run by women than by men named John."

—Justin Wolfers, "Fewer Women Run Big Companies Than Men Named John," *New York Times*

In a study of 360-degree feedback for 2,482 managers, Lawrence A. Pfaff & Associates found:

"The study, conducted over five years, shows significant differences in the leadership skill levels practiced by male and female managers. The study included 2,482 managers (1727 males, 755 females) from 459 organizations. It included managers at all levels.

"Employees rated female managers higher than male managers in seventeen of the twenty skill areas assessed, fifteen at a statistically significant level. Men and women tied in the other three areas. Bosses rated female managers higher than male managers in sixteen of the twenty skill areas, all sixteen at a statistically significant level. . . .

"'Our first two studies challenged the conventional wisdom that women are only better at the so called softer skills such as communicating, empowering people and being positive,' said Pfaff. 'This new study using data over a five-year period once again indicates that the conventional wisdom is wrong.' . . .

"'The statistical significance of this data is dramatic,' said Pfaff. 'Over a five-year period while gathering data on more than 2,400 subjects, on average, men are not rated significantly higher by any of the raters in any of the areas measured.'"

To Do: 5A   This topic has been of the utmost concern to me since 1996, when the president of my training company, Heather Shea, opened my eyes at a meeting she called on my account with an amazing group of women leaders, from giant companies, start-ups, education, and other areas. The research reported above is but the tip of the tip of the iceberg. The accumulated evidence regarding women's leadership effectiveness—and relative leadership effectiveness—merits the term "overwhelming." Hence my to-do here is simply to say that if you don't have at least that more or less balanced gender executive level leadership, you are beyond a shadow of doubt making a major strategic business effectiveness blunder.

And, by the way, my argument is about organizational effectiveness, not "social justice." While I think social justice is of surpassing importance and have tried to live my personal and professional life accordingly, it is not the primary topic under the microscope here.

Women's Negotiating Strengths

- *"Ability to put themselves in their counterparts' shoes*
- *Comprehensive, attentive and detailed communication style*
- *Empathy that facilitates trust-building*
- *Curious and active listeners*
- *Less competitive attitude*
- *Strong sense of fairness and ability to persuade*
- *Proactive risk manager*
- *Collaborative decision-making"*

—Horacio Falcão, "Say It Like a Woman: Why the 21st-Century Negotiator Will Need the Female Touch," *World Business*

Women Are Stellar Business Owners

"The growth and success of women-owned businesses is one of the most profound changes taking place in the business world today."

—Margaret Heffernan, *How She Does It: How Women Entrepreneurs Are Changing the Rules of Business Success*

More relevant data from Heffernan:

- U.S. firms owned or controlled by women: 10.4 million (40 percent of all firms).
- The number of American employees of women-owned businesses exceeds the total number of employees of the bellwether Fortune 500.
- Growth rate of women-owned firms vs. all firms: twice as high.
- Rate of jobs created by women-owned firms vs. all firms: twice as high.
- Likelihood of women-owned firms staying in business vs. all firms: greater than 1.0.
- Growth rate of women-owned companies with revenues of > $1,000,000 and > 100 employees vs. all firms: two times higher.

Women's Blue Ribbon Skills at Investment, from *Warren Buffett Invests Like a Girl: And Why You Should, Too*

- Trade less than men do
- Exhibit less overconfidence—more likely to know what they don't know
- Shun risk more than male investors do

- Are less optimistic, more realistic, than their male counterparts
- Put in more time and effort researching possible investments—consider details and alternate points of view
- Are more immune to peer pressure—tend to make decisions the same way regardless of who's watching
- Learn from their mistakes

—LouAnn Lofton, *Warren Buffett Invests Like a Girl: And Why You Should, Too*

"When women get involved in finances, they do better than men, because men focus on a shorter-term performance, while women take a longer view."

—Kathy Murphy, president, Fidelity Investments, manager of $1.7 trillion in assets, quoted in *TheStreet*

Women's Strengths Match New Economy Needs

Women: *". . .link rather than rank [workers]; favor interactive-collaborative leadership styles [empowerment beats top-down decision making]; are comfortable sharing information; see redistribution of power as victory, not surrender; readily accept ambiguity; honor intuition as well as rationality; are inherently flexible; appreciate cultural diversity."*

—Judy B. Rosener, summarized by Hilarie Owen, *Creating Leaders in the Classroom*

The positive assessment of women's leadership skills in general is likely to be far more pronounced given emerging changes in organizational structure and network structure. In ambiguous settings, where traditional, rigid hierarchy is no longer ubiquitous, women's demonstrated relative strengths are more important than ever.

To Do:
5B

- Women are better leaders.
- Women are better negotiators.
- Women are better business owners.
- Women are better investors.
- Women are better fit for new economy needs.

Consider carefully. Act accordingly. Start immediately.

Leadership / Women / COVID-19

It has been widely reported and commented upon that the nations that have best responded to the COVID-19 epidemic are all led by women. While the sample size is small, I am among those who do not think this outcome is without significance. (I even suggested on Twitter that no men should be CEOs of hospitals. Directionally, if not literally, I was in fact very serious.)

While there are very empathetic men and women with an empathy deficit, in general women have a disposition to exhibit more empathy and other "soft" (which are really "hard") traits.

Hence, relative to COVID-19, and issues of racial inequality, my argument for more women, at least an F-M 50-50 balance in senior leadership roles, is significantly strengthened.

1.6

Abiding Community Responsibility, Extreme Community Engagement

"Community" is a wondrous word. The dictionary definition that rings most true to me features the words "care about each other." Community, then, is indeed a word that first and foremost evokes "caring."

Think community and your business perspective moves far beyond the spreadsheet. Do superior work, sure, but superior work that emanates from a cooperative venture devoted to every member's flourishing. Moreover, organizations are communities embedded in the communities they and their employees occupy and the communities of their customers and vendors. In all manifestations, responsibility and care and concern should be hallmarks.

All of this is multiplied ten times—or a hundred times—as we face COVID-19 and our frayed social and political fabric. Simply put, today's noteworthy leaders will be those who put the nurturing of caring internal and external communities high on their daily, and strategic, agenda.

Interestingly, the best of the best has long understood this. In his superb book, *Small Giants: Companies That Choose to Be Great Instead of Big*, Bo Burlingham offers four pillars of small-giant success, the first of which is:

"Each company had an extraordinarily intimate relationship with the local city, town, or county in which it did business—a relationship that went well beyond the usual concept of 'giving back.'"

The lion's share of us pass our lives working in businesses—with employee populations that range from one to hundreds of thousands. Those businesses are, as noted, all embedded in communities. Hence, if you think clearly, businesses are not *part* of the community. Businesses *are* the community. And as such, and by definition, they have enormous direct and indirect community responsibilities—from decisions about environmental preservation and health care to support for schoolteachers and the school system and on and on. And that responsibility, to restate, has never been so obvious as at the moment of my writing.

What I am effectively demanding is a full-time, highly visible, enterprise commitment to Extreme Community Engagement. No Extreme Community Engagement, no excellence. Period.

Implications: how can the business strategy and everyday enterprise operational activities contribute directly to community development? Consider the following:

- Business executive team formal statement of commitment to Extreme Community Engagement.

- An advisory board of outsiders and insiders tasked with giving visibility to the company's community commitment and providing indirect oversight to internal community engagement activities.

- No decision of consequence—involving employees, facilities, products, customers served, suppliers used, communities affected—without a formal community impact analysis. The idea is ubiquity: community development / community partnership as explicit part of every decision, tiny as well as large, as it is contemplated and made.

- Extreme Community Engagement added to 100 percent of leaders' performance evaluations.

To Do: 6 There is no business excellence without community excellence. Think deeply about this. Do you accept my basic hypothesis? If not, why not? And if you do accept it, what concrete steps will you take to increase community engagement ASAP?

1.7

Universal Inclusivity:
Every Action,
Every Decision

"I appreciate your Black Lives Matter post. Now follow that up with a picture of your senior management team and your board."

—Brickson Diamond, CEO, diversity consulting firm Big Answers.

"I am ashamed to say I do not have a single Black employee who is at director level or above."

—Anne Wojcicki, CEO, 23andMe, in a company statement

Russell3000: 4.1 percent Black directors in 2019 (Black population 13.4 percent); 3.6 percent Black directors in 2008.

From a full-page *New York Times* statement by Omar Johnson, CEO, ØPUS United:

"Dear White corporate America . . .

I get it. I know you have the best intentions. . . . But the fact that you are only asking now is part of the problem. . . . You want to do the right thing. But you just don't know how. . . .

*For starters . . . listen. . . . Listen to your Black employees.
They have been sounding the alarm for years. But
don't stop there. Dig into the cold, hard data. Learn
where Black people exist in your company—and more
importantly, where they don't. Count the too few Black
faces in meetings. Notice the muted Black voices in
conversations where decisions are made. If you do that,
you'll see the problem clear as day. . . .*

What can I do?

*Inside your company walls, you need to hire more Black
people. Period.*

*On one side of the equation, that means fixing the
'pipeline' challenge, once and for all. So redouble your
efforts to recruit, attract, develop, and elevate Black
talent. Fund educational institutions that champion Black
kids and their futures.*

*On the other side of the equation, that means helping
Black talent climb the ladder, and turning over power
and authority to Black leaders. Retaining and promoting
are just as important as recruiting and hiring.*

*Analyze where you are as an organization. Set goals for
where you want to be. Put in place incentives to achieve
those goals. Measure them ruthlessly and relentlessly."*

To Do: Read it. Now. *Caste: The Origins of Our Discontent,* by Isabel
7A Wilkerson

Action. Now.

Injustice / inclusivity is not strategic.
Injustice / inclusivity is tactical, reflected in *every* recruiting and *every* hiring and *every* promotion and *every* evaluation decision.

Injustice / inclusivity is not about tomorrow.
Injustice / inclusivity is not about today.
Injustice / inclusivity is about now, looking around the real or virtual table at your next meeting, which starts 15 minutes from now.

Injustice / inclusivity is not about leadership.
Injustice / inclusivity is about studentship—reading and watching and talking and figuring out, individually and collectively, what you don't appreciate or observe or know, and a moving up the learning curve a step at a time.

To Do:
7B   You've got two eyes. Open them. Think about inclusivity. Now look around you. Can what you see pass the inclusivity test? Don't know the answer to that? Launch your oral / visual / print inclusivity studentship course today.

1.8

Managing Is the Pinnacle of Human Achievement

Managing, often as not, a pain in the ass. Somebody's got to do it: punching bag for higher-ups on one end, grouchy employees on the other; blame magnet if things go wrong, big bosses take the credit if things go right.

Or

Managing as it can / should be. The pinnacle of human achievement / the greatest life opportunity one can have; mid- to long-term success no more and no less than a function of one's dedication to and effectiveness at helping team members grow and flourish as individuals and as contributing members to an energetic, self-renewing organization dedicated to the relentless pursuit of excellence.

"Pinnacle of human achievement" may sound inflated, even absurd. However, it is an ironclad belief for me. Helping others grow—what could be more important, especially in these uncertain times? And, as usual in these pages, it turns out to be the most surefire way to produce growth and profitability.

Discuss at length the "pinnacle of human achievement." Is that too grand? If so, what's the alternative? What do you think *is* the apex of the leader's role? Is "leaders are 100 percent in the people business" accurate? In general? For you, personally? As reflected in your work today? This week?

First Things Before First Things

Ingest and act vigorously on these "First Things Before First Things" and I will be beside myself with joy and you will be many steps down the path to excellence:

- Hard (numbers / plans / org charts) is soft. Soft (people / relationships / culture) is hard.
- Hiring: soft skills, EQ first, 100 percent of jobs.
- Training: Enterprise Capital Investment #1.
- Frontline leaders are Corporate Strength #1.
- Women rule (or should).
- Abiding community responsibility, Extreme Community Engagement.
- Universal inclusivity: every action, every decision.
- Managing is the pinnacle of human achievement.

2

Excellence Is the
Next Five Minutes
(or Not)

2.9

Excellence Is the Next Five Minutes (or Not)

"We don't remember the days, we remember the moments."
—Cesare Pavese, poet

Excellence is not an "aspiration." Excellence is not a "hill to climb." Excellence is the next five minutes. (Or it is nothing at all.)

Excellence is your next five-minute conversation in the real or virtual "hallway."
Or not.

Excellence is your next email or text message. (This is sooooo true!!! Give me a collection of a leader's last 10 emails—and I'll give you an accurate assessment of his or her character and effectiveness.)
Or not.

Excellence is the first three minutes of your next meeting.
Or not.

Excellence is shutting up and listening—really listening / "aggressively" listening.
Or not.

Excellence is sending flowers to the hospital where your top customer's Mom is having serious surgery.
Or not.

Excellence is saying "Thank you" for something "small."
Or not.

Excellence is pulling out all the stops at warp speed to respond to a "minor" screw-up.
Or not.

Excellence is the flowers you bring to work on a dispiriting rainy day.
Or not.

Excellence is learning the names and school year of all 14 of your team members' kids.
Or not.

Excellence is bothering to learn the way folks in finance (or IS or Purchasing) think.
Or not.

Excellence is waaaay "over"-preparing for a three-minute presentation.
Or not.

What is Excellence? Perhaps 100 people will have 100 different ideas. Fair enough. But this is my book—and I want to lobby for what to me is the most meaningful definition of and approach to Excellence. In *In Search of Excellence*, we defined Excellence in terms of long-term performance. But that begs a / *the* question. How do you achieve that long-term super-effectiveness? And I strongly and passionately— and dogmatically—insist that the core, the bedrock of those standout long-term results, is indeed the five-minute real or virtual / by phone conversation in the "hall" you had right after the meeting ended an hour ago; and the seven-line email for which you are about to push the 'send' button.

Bottom line:

Did that passing five-minute conversation "reek of thoughtfulness?

Did you, leader, spend 80 percent of your last "conversation" . . . listening? (If so . . . are you really really sure it's 80 percent?)

Did that listening translate into 100 percent attentiveness ("fierce listening," according to author Susan Scott, quoted later)?

Was the tone positive (research demonstrates that positive acts are . . . 30 times . . . more powerful than negative-tinged acts or comments)?

And add it up:

Was or was not that brief conversation hurried, distracted, and emotionally empty? Or was it the exemplification of the Excellence that generates engaged employees aiming for the moon in their efforts, that, in turn, creates the long-term superior performance (innovation, peerless quality, breathtaking design, community engagement, "bottom line" results, etc.)?

Same-same with, yes (damn it!), a seven-line email:

Is it typo free—how else teach / model Excellence in Execution?

Does it begin with a greeting: "Hi Kai," "Hi Ana" that conveys personalization and civility, or is it brusque to the point of inhuman?

Do requests include, for instance, "Thank you in advance"?
Are the words and tone consistent with our corporate culture?

"Over the top," you say.
Think again, I say:

Excellent?
(Or not?)

Well this is indeed my book—and I therefore beg you to join me in the crusade for Excellence-as-imbedded-in-our-moment-to-moment-activities. Oh, and Excellence-is-the-next-five-minutes is, my anecdotal evidence suggests, a real upper in general. It sure as hell is for me, though I am hardly suggesting that I hit the mark anything like 100 percent of the time.

To Do: 9A Take your time on this. Please don't brush past it. What precisely does Excellence mean to you? (Please use practical examples.) What does Excellence mean to your peers? (Please please please try to reach agreement on this.)

To Do: 9B And if you buy my five-minute act, then practice deep breathing. (I'm not a meditator, so I'm not pushing a point of view.) By "practice deep breathing," I mean pause to consider:

Focus on "Listening Fiercely" in the meeting I'm about to walk or Zoom into. Don't interrupt. Ever.

Respond positively noticeably to any reported effort to "push the envelope," even a little bit.

Ensure that my positive responses outnumber my negative responses at least 5:1.

Pause before hitting the "send" button and reflect on the quality of the email. (That wee email reflects who I am as a human being. Do I like what I see?)

If face to face (F2F), religiously make eye contact as I walk down the hall.
And. . . .
And. . . .
(Excellent? Or not?)

2.10

Excellence: Organizational Performance

The Business of Human Betterment

"Business exists to enhance human wellbeing."

—Mihaly Csikszentmihalyi, *Good Business: Leadership, Flow, and the Making of Meaning* (the author is best known for his book *Flow: The Psychology of Optimal Experience*)

"Business was originated to produce happiness, not pile up millions."

—B.C. Forbes, first issue of *Forbes*, September 1917

"Enhance human wellbeing" sounds like a lofty idea and the ultimate abstraction. But given the changes racing down the road toward us, business has no less than a *requirement* to aim to live up to Mihaly Csikszentmihalyi's challenge.

Let's pause here. I think the ideas herein are no less than today's survival ideas. NOT OPTIONAL. But I must add: What is suggested in these pages is a satisfying way to live, a way you can be proud of, a contribution to your community. Yes, the dollars in must exceed the dollars out. But there is a heck of a lot more to life than producing and then pouring over the next spreadsheet. Suppose I own a grocery store. It's a tough business, in general, and especially with Covid-19 and that Amazon truck (drone?) hovering nearby. But my real thrill comes from my frontline employees who got boosts from me and went on to solid careers. My real thrill is standing several feet from the check-out and listening to 45 seconds of friendly banter between an engaged and cheerful checkout clerk and a customer whose day is brightened a bit by that banter. That's the point, isn't it? (And more: See below on Extreme Humanism. That banter between the clerk and the customer is akin to a tiny mirror mounted on an MRI machine that allows eye contact with the nurse and thence radically alters, for the better, the patient's experience. Multiplied a hundred or a thousand times, it is a Big-League Strategic Differentiator that spurs business success. And makes you feel good about what you are doing during your short time on earth.)

Enterprise Excellence:
People (Leaders) Serving
People (the Frontline Team) Serving
People (Customers / Communities)

Organizational EXCELLENCE = People (leaders / managers) Serving People (our team members) Serving People (our customers and communities).

—inspired by Robert Greenleaf's *Servant Leadership: A Journey Into the Nature of Legitimate Power and Greatness*

Enterprise Excellence is about just two things: *People. Service.* Excellence = Service. Service to one's teammates, service to one's customers and vendors, service to our communities. In a sense, service to humanity, per Csikszentmihalyi above, in some small way.

"Business exists to enhance human wellbeing." This damn sentence rolls around and around and around in my head. I really really really buy it. Do you? Do your colleagues? What precisely does this mean in terms of today's activities? Have I / we positively contributed to human wellbeing today? I am fully aware that your day has been about one-damn-thing-after-another. That's the problem—and the opportunity. Is your human-wellbeing-meter turned on? Are you reflecting on this grand aspiration, which can only be exhibited—or not—in your and your team's next micro-action?

2.11

Excellence: People
Really First

Moral Management / Moral Obligation

"Almost half of U.S. jobs are at high risk of computerization over the next 20 years, according to Oxford academics Carl Benedikt Frey and Michael A. Osborne."

—Harriet Taylor, "How Robots Will Kill the 'Gig Economy,'" CNBC

"The root of our problem is not that we're in a Great Recession or a Great Stagnation, but rather that we are in the early throes of a Great Restructuring. Our technologies are racing ahead, but our skills and organizations are lagging behind."

—Erik Brynjolfsson and Andrew McAfee, *Race AGAINST the Machine*

Action translation . . .

Your principal moral obligation as a leader is to develop the skillset of every one of the people in your charge – temporary as well as semi-permanent – to the maximum extent of your abilities and consistent with their 'revolutionary' needs in the years ahead. (Bonus: This is also the #1 mid- to long-term growth and profit maximization strategy!)

This is my suggested (required!) contemporary leader's "do or die" Formal Credo in the age of runaway AI, etc.

Excellence / Moral Management / Not

Polls from all around the world are astonishingly consistent: 75 percent to 85 percent of people (workers) are unhappy with or disconnected from their job. (For example, see Gallup's 2016 "The Worldwide Employee Engagement Crisis.") Sure, there's the increasing technological pressure or the impact of, say, a product that goes bust (for example, Boeing's 737 MAX). But such factors need not, should not!, keep a manager from creating a supportive, humane, personal-growth driven environment.

Creating a positive and engaging work environment, regardless of circumstances and especially in crappy circumstances, is how managers earn their pay.

In fact, the premier mark of a great leader is precisely to create and maintain a spirited, effective, supportive environment when the world around her is in flames (as it is, in effect, as I write). Not mercilessly pushing short-term financial goals in the midst of a shitstorm, but exhibiting true camaraderie and compassion and care when things are at their worst. (FYI: As I see it, 75 percent disengaged workers on a team is a felonious "leader" offense.)

To Do:
11

This is personal to me. Are you and your fellow leaders willing to "sign up" for: "Your principal moral obligation as a leader is to develop the skillset of every one of the people in your charge . . . to the maximum extent of your abilities. . ."?

FYI: Your answer to that question determines whether I have wasted my time—or not—over the last 40+ years. Hint: I am not kidding.

2.12

The Bedrock of Excellence: Investing (Big Time, All the Time) in Relationships

"The capacity to develop close and enduring relationships is one mark of a leader. Unfortunately, many leaders of major companies believe their job is to create the strategy, organization structure and organizational processes. Then they just delegate the work to be done, remaining aloof from the people doing the work."

—Bill George, former CEO, Medtronic, *Authentic Leadership: Rediscovering the Secrets to Creating Lasting Value*

"Allied commands depend on mutual confidence and this confidence is gained, above all through the development of friendships."

—General Dwight D. Eisenhower, from the magazine *Armchair General*, which features leadership "secrets" from the most renowned officers. ("Perhaps [DDE's] most outstanding ability [at West Point] was the ease with which he made friends and earned the trust of fellow cadets who came from widely varied backgrounds; it was a quality that would pay great dividends during his future coalition command.") Eisenhower's World War II success featured an extraordinary ability to keep (VERY!) fractious Allies on more or less the same page.

"Personal relationships are the fertile soil from which all advancement, all success, all achievement in real life grow."

—Ben Stein, investment guru

Best relationships win ("the fertile soil from which *all* advancement, *all* success, *all* achievement in real life grow"). But as Bill George suggests, a lot (most???) leaders "don't get it." They would doubtless agree that "relationships are important." But they would fall short of a necessary passion / obsession with investing in and building and maintaining relationships.

Yes:
Passion.
Obsession.
Investment.

There are no—none, zero—shortcuts.
EXCELLENT relationships take time.
Gobs and gobs of time.
And that is as true as ever right now.

To Do: 12A	What—precisely—Is your formal RIS / Relationship Investment Strategy? For today? For the week? For the month? Relationship development epitomizes the "Soft is Hard" idea. Hence, I suggest (DEMAND—I guess I can't give an order, but I wish I could) a formal plan for your ongoing investment in relationships. And I suggest that you "demand" such a plan from every leader—and, in fact, non-leader—in the organization.
To Do: 12B	Clearly and measurably demonstrated EXCELLENCE in relationship development should be Test #1 for promotion into any leadership slot. (For example, test the quality of each candidate's network within and beyond her or his unit.)

2.13

Excellence: SMEs / Small- and Medium-Sized Enterprises

Employers Nonpareil / Innovators Nonpareil

"I am often asked by would-be entrepreneurs seeking escape from life within huge corporate structures, 'How do I build a small firm for myself?' The answer seems obvious: Buy a very large one and just wait."
—Paul Ormerod, *Why Most Things Fail: Evolution, Extinction and Economics*

"Mr. Foster and his McKinsey colleagues collected detailed performance data stretching back 40 years for 1,000 U.S. companies. They found that none of the long-term survivors in this group managed to outperform the market. Worse, the longer companies had been in the database, the worse they did."
—Simon London, "Long-term survival of the not so fit," *Financial Times*

Fact is, the giants perform poorly over the long haul. In Foster's research: zero of a 1,000 beat the market over a four-decade period. The saving grace for employment and the U.S. economy (and everybody's economy)? SMEs!

"Research shows that new, small companies create almost all the new private sector jobs—and are disproportionately innovative."

—Gervais Williams, superstar fund manager, "If Small is the Future then We Will All Be Big Winners," *Financial Times*

The management "guru" gang—*including me!*—mostly act as if the business world consists of the Fortune 500 and the FTSE 100. In fact, the lion's share of us, well over 80 percent, labor in mostly unsung Small- and Medium-sized Enterprises / SMEs. SMEs-Are-Us.

Nothing excites me more than Unabashed Excellence in an arena that others write off as boring in an oddball corner of the world. For example, on the main street of the tiny town of Motueka, New Zealand (near my New Zealand cottage), you will find a nondescript door leading to the operations office and factory of family-run W.A. Coppins, which by most accounts is the unabashed global leader in designing and building sea anchors and related products. Coppins' demanding customers include the U.S. Navy and the Government of Norway. (Tiny world-beaters like Coppins make me [literally] giggle with delight.)

FYI / Family-run businesses USA (according to "Family Businesses Contribution to the U.S. Economy: A Closer Look" from Kennesaw State University):

64% *GDP.*
62% *total employment.*
78% *new job creation.*

" . . . agile creatures darting between the legs of the multinational monsters"

—"Germany's Growth: New Rules, Old Companies," *Bloomberg BusinessWeek* on the effectiveness of German mid-size superstars, the Mittelstand companies. Germany's niche-dominating mid-sized companies are the unquestioned engine of the country's peerless export success.

Attributes of SME Excellence, courtesy Bo Burlingham, *Small Giants: Companies That Chose to Be Great Instead of Big*:

"1. They cultivated exceptionally intimate relationships with customers and suppliers, based on personal contact, one-on-one interaction, and mutual commitment to delivering on promises. . . .

2. Each company had an extraordinarily intimate relationship with the local city, town, or county in which it did business—a relationship that went well beyond the usual concept of 'giving back.' . . .

3. The companies had what struck me as unusually intimate workplaces. . . .

4. I noticed the passion that the leaders brought to what the company did. They loved the subject matter, whether it be music, safety lighting, food, special effects, constant torque hinges, beer, records storage, construction, dining, or fashion."

Observe that the success factors are *all* so-called *"soft"* attributes.

SME Superstars / Inspiring Reading

Small Giants: Companies That Chose to Be Great Instead of Big, by Bo Burlingham

Simply Brilliant: How Great Organizations Do Ordinary Things in Extraordinary Ways, by William Taylor

The Healing Organization: Awakening the Conscience of Business to Help Save the World, by Raj Sisodia and Michael Gelb

The Passion Economy: The New Rules for Thriving in the Twenty-First Century, by Adam Davidson

Retail Superstars: Inside the 25 Best Independent Stores in America, by George Whalin

To Do: 13 If learning is your goal, and I assume it is or you wouldn't be here, seek out, in print and in "real life," magical small / smallish firms and study them and learn from them. It's particularly important to go beyond your field of business—or comfort. For example, a restaurateur learning from a hospital ICU, or vice versa, and so on. Studenthood is always a winning strategy!!!

2.14

Excellence: Enough

Vanguard Funds founder, the late Jack Bogle, father of no load / fee index funds and arguably America's most successful investor for decades, wrote a brilliant book titled *Enough: True Measures of Money, Business, and Life*. It begins with this vignette:

"At a party given by a billionaire on Shelter Island, Kurt Vonnegut informs his pal, Joseph Heller, that their host, a hedge fund manager, had made more money in a single day than Heller had earned from his wildly popular novel Catch-22 over its whole history. Heller responds . . . 'Yes, but I have something he will never have . . . enough.'"

The heart of Bogle's book is captured by the chapter titles:

"Too Much Cost, Not Enough Value"
"Too Much Speculation, Not Enough Investment"
"Too Much Complexity, Not Enough Simplicity"
"Too Much Counting, Not Enough Trust"
"Too Much Business Conduct, Not Enough Professional Conduct"
"Too Much Salesmanship, Not Enough Stewardship"
"Too Much Management, Not Enough Leadership"
"Too Much Focus on Things, Not Enough Focus on Commitment"
"Too Many Twenty-First Century Values, Not Enough Eighteenth-Century Values"
"Too Much 'Success,' Not Enough Character"

(FYI One of my thrills-of-a-lifetime was being invited to write the foreword to the paperback edition of *Enough*.)

To Do: Read the book! Reflect: How does this apply to my day-to-day
14 professional life—in particular, the kind of organization I'd like
to build?

2.15

Excellence: Not Enough

Milton Friedman as the "Anti-Bogle": Friedman's "Maximize Shareholder Value" Fiasco / 1970–???

A Few Examples:

#1: "In 1970," Duff McDonald reports in his book *The Golden Passport*, "Nobel Prize–winning economist Milton Friedman published an essay in the *New York Times Magazine* titled 'The Social Responsibility of Business Is to Increase Its Profits.'"

Friedman's article was the start of the age of shareholder value maximization. I titled a recent explanatory essay, "Maximizing Shareholder Value: The Morally Bankrupt, Incomparably Destructive (Not Legally Required) Economic Idea That Decapitated Modern Business and Is Spurring Social Instability." Well, that is what I believe—even if it makes for a wordy title!

#2: William Lazonick, in a *Harvard Business Review* article titled "Profits Without Prosperity," lays out the quantitative case against shareholder value maximization:

"The very people we rely on to make investments in the productive capabilities that will increase our shared prosperity are instead devoting most of their companies' profit to uses that will increase their own prosperity."

Consider this from "Profits Without Prosperity":

449 S&P 500 companies publicly listed 2003-2012:
91% of $2.4 trillion earnings were used for stock buybacks and dividends
9% left was used for "productive capabilities or higher incomes for employees"

That "productive capabilities" share—9% in 2012—was 50% prior to the launch of Friedman's pernicious movement.

(Mind-boggling / Nightmare-inducing) Translation:

1970: 50%: Workers / R&D / Productive Investments Strategy: "retain and re-invest."

2012: 9%: Workers / R&D / Productive Investments Strategy: "downsize and distribute"

#3: The worm may be starting to turn. Harvard Business School all-time great professor Joseph Bower and Lynn Paine, write in "The Error at the Heart of Corporate Leadership," *HBR*:

"The time has come to challenge the model of corporate governance. Its mantra of maximizing shareholder value is distracting companies / leaders from the innovation, strategic renewal and investment in the future that require their attention. History has shown that with enlightened management and sensible regulation, companies can play a useful role in helping society adapt to constant change. But that can only happen if directors and managers have sufficient discretion to take a longer, broader view of the company and its business. As long as they face the prospect of a surprise attack by unaccountable 'owners,' today's business leaders have little choice but to focus on the here and now."

#4: Rejecting Short-Term Shareholder Value Maximization And Playing The "Long Game" / The Payoff Is Stupendous

Dominic Barton, Managing Director of McKinsey, James Manyika, Sarah Keohane Williamson, "The Data: Where Long-Termism Pays Off," *Harvard Business Review*:

"Seeking to quantify the effects of short-termism at the company level and to assess its cumulative impact on the nation's economy, we tracked data on 615 nonfinancial U.S. companies from 2001 to 2014 (representing 60% to 65% of total U.S. market cap). We used several standard metrics as proxies for long-term behavior, including the ratio of capital expenditures to depreciation (a measure of investment), accruals as a share of revenue (an indicator of earnings quality), and margin growth. To ensure valid results and avoid bias in our sample, we

compared companies only to industry peers with similar opportunity sets and market conditions. Adjusting for company size and industry, we identified 167 companies (about 27% of the total set) that had a long-term orientation."

Results from Barton et al.:
2001–2015: Long-term Investors vs. All Others:

Average Company Revenue: +47%
Average Company Earnings: +36%
Average Company Economic Profit: +81%
Average Market Capitalization: +58%
Average Job Creation: +132%

U-N-E-Q-U-I-V-O-C-A-L!!!
Re-read especially: +132%

To Do:
15

Not many readers are CEOs of giant publicly traded firms. So how does this apply to us mortals? To some extent, it is the ultimate expansion of "Hard is soft. Soft is hard." The story here: Short-termism is a snare and a delusion, and destructive of individuals and society as a whole. Investment for the mid- to long-term, particularly investment in people and innovation, pays off for workers and customers and communities and . . . on the "bottom line." And this people / innovation / long-term view applies as much (or more!) to a local Nine-Person Plumbing-Services Company as to a Corporate Giant. Do a serious self-examination relative to these ideas and this data and your world.

2.16

Excellence Is a Way of Life

Excellence Is Spiritual

Business Excellence Is About Who We Are and How We Contribute

EXCELLENCE, by my definition, is first and foremost a way of life, a way of behaving with care and respect toward our fellow human beings and our communities day in and day out—moment in and moment out.

EXCELLENCE is, in an important way, spiritual.

Frankly, I normally avoid terms such as "spiritual." After all, my shtick is practical, down-to-earth analysis and actionable advice. What else from a double-degreed engineering graduate? But as I reflect on the power of Excellence—especially in these chaotic times—it is clear to me that the message I want to leave you with could be uttered from behind a church pulpit. Work is how we spend most of our waking hours, and it is, then, by definition "who we are." And who we are as leaders is how we contribute, down deep, to the wellbeing of our mates. Hence, I throw my reluctance aside and wholeheartedly embrace the "spiritual" essence of Excellence! I remember with delight getting a letter from a Catholic priest—I was raised Presbyterian—informing me that his theology Ph.D. thesis at Notre Dame University was based on *In Search of Excellence*. As I recall, I teared up.

As mentioned previously, less than 10 percent of us work for the Fortune 500 or giant enterprises. However, overall, the lion's share of us work for a business of some sort. So, effectively, the state-of-business is the state-of-the community / country / world. A discussion of business, then, is a discussion of, though it might sound grandiose, the quality of civilization itself. And, therefore, Business Excellence is of the utmost importance.

To Do:
16

This is your life we are talking about!

Business Excellence (in my considered opinion) is about who we are and how we contribute, and therefore a million miles beyond abstract balance sheets.

I introduced the word "EXCELLENCE" into my business lexicon years ago, while, coincidentally, drafting a presentation soon after having attended a soaring, uplifting performance by the San Francisco Ballet. What went through my mind was something like, "Why can't business be like the ballet?"

"Business Excellence."
A way of being.
This book is my "last hurrah."
Are you with me?

3

Strategy Is a Commodity

Execution Is an Art

3.17

Execution: "Can Do" / The "Last 95 Percent"

"CAN DO. The Difficult We Do Now. The Impossible Takes a Little Longer."
—Motto of the United States Navy Seabees

My first leadership training ground, Vietnam, 1966-1968. The Seabees ("Seabees" is derived from "CB" / Construction Battalion) are the Navy's fabled, no-BS, no polished shoes, combat construction force, born at Guadalcanal in 1942. Their role is indeed to do the impossible. For example, build and complete an airstrip on Guadalcanal, from scratch, in 13 days, under fire, with lousy equipment, in hopelessly rocky terrain and, to top it off, during a monsoon. That spirit, and similar results, remain the Seabee trademark at, now, age 79.

"Don't forget execution, boys. It's the all-important last 95 percent."
—*McKinsey Director*

A McKinsey Director (most senior rank) stuck his head into a conference room in San Francisco and shouted from the door to my teammates and me, "Don't forget execution, boys. It's the all-important last 95 percent." He's right of course, and, later in my career, the whole impetus for the McKinsey study that produced *In Search of Excellence* was a command to me from the firm's overall Managing Director to focus on execution, or the lack thereof. "Tom," he said, "we design these extraordinary strategies, yet the client can't implement. What's the disconnect?" Time and again, in enterprises of all flavors, problem analysis rules the roost and execution is taken for granted. And it is, in fact, the "last 95 percent."

To Do:
17

Common refrain: "A leader draws people to her side with an inspiring vision. And she needs a manager to handle the details." Well, I'll take the "manager." You can have and keep the "leader." A good book does not come from a fabulous idea—it comes from two years of exhausting research and seven or eight or 12 (or 20) complete re-writes. So, my advice is: Forget the glamour and the abstractions. Focus on getting something, anything, concrete done by the end of the day. And if you're in charge, recruit for your team some un-flashy people who are not happy unless their hands are dirty.

3.18

Execution:
Conrad Hilton and
Tucked-In Shower Curtains

"Late in his life, Conrad Hilton appeared on 'The Tonight Show.' Host Johnny Carson asked whether he had a message for the American people about what he'd learned in building his hotel empire. Hilton paused, then turned to the camera. 'Please,' he said, 'remember to tuck the shower curtain inside the tub.'"

—Deborah Aarts, *Canadian Business*

This Hilton-ism has been the first slide in virtually every presentation I've given in the last five years. In the hotel business, "location location location" (and a great architect) matter; they entice me through the door for my first visit. But it's the likes of that tucked in shower curtain (×100) that bring me back and induce me to recommend the hotel to my friends. And as businesspeople know so well, you typically lose money on the first transactions and rake in the cash on transactions #18, #19, #20—and via that vital (and one hopes viral) word of mouth and social media.

(FYI: There's another twist of surpassing importance beneath the surface of the Hilton story. If shower-curtain tucking matters most, then the shower-curtain tuckers are the most important people on the staff, which is in wild contrast with the typical treatment of this group. More on that in Topic #4.)

To Do: 18	Let someone else recruit the MBAs. The winning-strategy-for-life is to obsess on the people who tuck in the shower curtains. Look back on the last full working day. How much time did you spend on / with your organization's "shower curtain tuckers"? (Ask yourself that at the end of every work day.)

3.19

Execution: Keep it Simple / Execution Is Strategy / The Iron Law of Execution

Keep it Simple

"Costco figured out the big, simple things and executed with total fanaticism."

—Charles Munger, Vice Chairman, Berkshire Hathaway

Costco's results have been exceptional—and those results are built significantly on their abiding and obvious regard for their frontline employees who do the real day-to-day work of the organization (i.e., "execute fanatically").

Execution *Is* Strategy

"Execution IS strategy."
—Fred Malek

Malek was my White House / OMB boss in 1973–74. Fred did not deal in abstractions. He wanted results. Now. No ruffles, no flourishes, and, God knows, no excuses. (For example, I once did a Washington D.C.-Bangkok round trip in 48 hours to deliver a brief message to our ambassador in a 15-minute meeting; Fred said "face-to-face;" I did face-to-face. Period. FYI: It worked. The formerly skeptical ambassador supported a critical program we were considering.)

"Execution is the job of the business leader. . . . When assessing candidates, the first things I look for was energy and enthusiasm for execution. . . . Does she talk about the thrill of getting things done, or does she keep wandering back to strategy or philosophy? Does she detail the obstacles that she had to overcome? Does she explain the roles played by the people assigned to her?"
—Larry Bossidy with Ram Charan, *Execution: The Discipline of Getting Things Done*

To Do:
19A
Religiously apply the "Bossidy Rule" to your hiring and promoting practices.

The Iron Law of Execution

"Execution is a systematic process of rigorously discussing hows and whats, tenaciously following through, and ensuring accountability."

—Larry Bossidy with Ram Charan, *Execution: The Discipline of Getting Things Done*

THE IRON LAW: When you talk all the time about execution, it's likely to happen. When you don't, it doesn't.

Q: "Could it be this simple?"
A: "To a significant degree, yes."

To Do: 19B Make this your personal Iron Law: In every conversation and every meeting, the execution / implementation / who-what-when-next milestones discussion should be front and center and dominant (for example, 15 to-do slides in a 30-slide PowerPoint presentation) and reiterated more or less immediately and ever thereafter in follow-up communications. Obsess on execution and make your obsession public knowledge.

Execution / The Last Word(s)

For want of a nail, the shoe was lost,
For want of a shoe, the horse was lost,
For want of a horse, the rider was lost,
For want of a rider, the message was lost,
For want of a message, the battle was lost,
For want of a battle, the war was lost,
For want of a war, the kingdom fell,
And all for the want of a nail.

Source: Thirteenth-century proverb

"Strategy is a commodity, execution is an art."

—Peter Drucker

"Amateurs talk about strategy. Professionals talk about logistics."

—General R.H. Barrow, USMC

"Blame nobody.
  Expect nothing.
  Do something."

—Bill Parcells, NFL coach

People *Really* First

"Business Has to Give People Enriching, Rewarding Lives . . . or It's Simply Not Worth Doing."

The Excellence Dividend appeared in 2018. Publicity mostly consisted of podcasts. Perhaps 20. With one exception, the questioner was well prepared and fun to talk to. But there was one odd thing. I'd bet that in fifteen of the 20 cases, this question, almost word for word, was asked as the opener:

"Tom, you talk a lot about people, why is that?"

The unexpurgated response I wanted to give was, "What the f--- else is there to talk about?"
(without the ---)

Business is about people.
People first.
People second.
People . . .
People last.
Period.

So . . .

4.20

People *Really* First

Becoming More Than They Have Ever Dreamed of Being

"Business has to give people enriching, rewarding lives . . . or it's simply not worth doing."

—Richard Branson, *Business Stripped Bare: Adventures of a Global Entrepreneur*

This is the text on Slide #1 of 4,096 in my 27 chapter PowerPoint "summa" at excellencenow.com. Needless to say, the choice was not easy. But, years later, I have never wavered: #1 / 4,096 = #1 / 4,096.

Definition: A great manager is literally *desperate* to have each of their team members succeed and grow and flourish.

To Do:
20A   So . . . are you Ms. / Mr. Boss . . . D-E-S-P-E-R-A-T-E?????? (My word choice is *very* deliberate.)

"No matter what the situation, [the great manager's] first response is always to think about the individual concerned and how things can be arranged to help that individual experience success."

—Marcus Buckingham, *The One Thing You Need to Know About Great Managing, Great Leading, and Sustained Individual Success* (There is no one in this arena whom I respect more than Marcus Buckingham.)

"The role of the Director is to create a space where the actors and actresses can become more than they have ever been before, more than they've dreamed of being."

—Robert Altman, Director

To Do: Reflect on Mr. Altman's precise word choice:
20B

"More than they have ever been before"
"More than they dreamed of being"

Lovely words. YES. But please consider the exact meaning of those words and, if you are a leader, do they square—use the exact words above—with your view of your role? (And your actions in the last 24 hours??)

From Robert Greenleaf's book, *Servant Leadership*, these are questions leaders must ask concerning the people on their team:

"Do those served grow as persons?

Do they, while being served, become healthier, wiser, freer, more autonomous, more likely themselves to become servants?"

Reflect on the term, "Servant Leadership" and read, if per chance you haven't, Greenleaf's peerless book!

"If you want the staff to give great service to customers, the leaders have to give great service to the staff."

—Ari Weinzweig, co-founder of Zingerman's, *A Lapsed Anarchist's Approach to Building a Great Business*

So apparently simple. so very often overlooked. If this were the norm, I wouldn't need to write this book. In fact, I don't "need" to write this book. *I have to write this book.* This is my last shot at convincing you to do what I'd call the obvious: for example, "give great service to staff."

"What employees experience, Customers will. . .
Your Customers will never be any happier than
your employees."

—John DiJulius, on his Customer Experience blog

Profound.

(Yes, it merits the word "profound." I guess it's also a "profound" comment to point out how many so-called smart people "don't get it.")

If you want to WOW the customer, first you must WOW the people who WOW the customer.

From me: And I admit to a near-addiction to the word "Wow."

To Do:
20C
So have you "WOWed" your work team today? (And, damn it, please use the word "WOW.")

"When I hire someone, that's when I go to work for them."

—John DiJulius, *The Relationship Economy: Building Stronger Customer Connections in the Digital Age*

To Do: **20D**	Remind yourself every morning when you walk through the office door or attend your first Zoom meeting: I work for them—not vice versa.

"I didn't have a 'mission statement' at Burger King. I had a dream. Very simple. It was something like, 'Burger King is 250,000 people, every one of whom gives a shit.' Every one. Accounting. Systems. Not just the drive through. Everyone is 'in the brand.' That's what we're talking about, nothing less."

—Barry Gibbons, former Burger King CEO, turnaround superstar

"What I'm trying to do as the leader of Tangerine is to build a culture in which individuals—people—have the means to truly thrive. To succeed. To be happy in their work. To feel fulfilled and growing. A culture that gives voice to all team members. Why? Because being good to your own people is good business. When Me thrives, We benefit. And so the title of this book is Weology. What I call 'Weology' is about creating win-win scenarios. It's a way of putting people first in the short term so that a company can thrive in the long term. . . . The calculation is that numbers don't have to rule the way a business—not even a bank—is run . . . People who are happy in their work make the best kind of ambassadors for our company, our corporate culture, because they live Weology and know it's true."

—Peter Aceto, CEO, Tangerine, from *Weology: How Everybody Wins When We Comes Before Me* (Tangerine is an innovative, very successful Canadian financial services corporation.)

"An organization can only become the-best-version-of-itself to the extent that the people who drive that organization are striving to become better-versions-of-themselves. . . . Our employees are our first customers, and our most important customers."

—Matthew Kelly, *The Dream Manager*

Matthew Kelly's point, in a book based on a housekeeping services organization, is that every employee has a dream, often *not* directly job related (for example, a small step forward educationally for a part-time housekeeper). And leadership that helps that employee realize their dream will be rewarded with superior performance and will also have behaved in general as an integral part of the larger community.

To Do:
20E

Are you in the "Employee Dream Fulfillment" business? Yes, it's a mouthful, and I don't imagine you'll respond with 100 percent buy in. But the logic is impeccable. So do me the honor of thinking seriously about "dream fulfillment" and consider reading Mr. Kelly's book.

"We are ladies and gentlemen serving ladies and gentlemen."

—From the Ritz-Carlton Credo

In the hotel business, members of frontline staff have historically been treated more like cannon fodder than "ladies and gentlemen". This mark of respect ("we are ladies and gentlemen . . ."), certified as a written core belief, is a (Very) Big Deal. (FYI: The Ritz-Carlton is, beyond its P&L results, routinely voted one of the best companies to work for in America.)

"The path to a hostmanship culture paradoxically does not go through the guest. . . . True hostmanship leaders focus first on their employees. . . . We went through the hotel [immediately upon acquiring it] and made a . . . 'consideration renovation.' Instead of redoing bathrooms, dining rooms, and guest rooms, we gave employees new uniforms, bought flowers and fruit, and changed colors. Our focus was totally on the staff. They were the ones we wanted to make happy. We wanted them to wake up every morning excited about a new day at work."

—Jan Gunnarsson and Olle Blohm, authors, management "gurus"—*and* hotel owners.

To Do:
20F

"Consideration Renovation" is an inspired term. How about it??? (And what might your "Consideration Renovation" look like? Details, please!)

The Patient Comes Second

"Nobody comes home after a surgery saying, 'Man, that was the best suturing I've ever seen!" or 'Sweet, they took out the correct kidney!' Instead, we talk about the people who took care of us, the ones who coordinated the whole procedure—everyone from the receptionist to the nurses to the surgeon. And we don't just tell stories around the dinner table. We share our experiences through conversations with friends and colleagues and via social media sites like Facebook and Twitter."

—Paul Spiegelman and Britt Berrett, from the chapter "What Does Come First?" in *Patients Come Second: Leading Change by Changing the Way You Lead*

Joy, Inc.

"It may sound radical, unconventional, and bordering on being a crazy business idea. However—as ridiculous as it sounds—joy is the core belief of our workplace. Joy is the reason my company, Menlo Innovations, a custom software design and development firm in Ann Arbor [MI], exists. It defines what we do and how we do it. It is the single shared belief of our entire team."

—Richard Sheridan, *Joy, Inc.: How We Built a Workplace People Love*

Menlo is the "real deal." This is not pie-in-the-sky. It took me a while to buy in, but today, having visited Menlo, I am a "raving fan." As usual, this requires more than a quick read. "Joy" will, I suspect, be a stretch for most readers. But why-the-hell-not? (And, as usual, 100 percent of the time, in this section, this is also a close-to-guaranteed profit generator.)

To Do: 20G Dream fulfillment. Hostmanship. Joy, Inc. These are extraordinary words, and I've been piling on with as many such terms as possible. I hope to make my point with extreme language and repetition.

People *Really* First:
The Client That Had to Be Fired

"I've come to resign your business, because your Executive Vice President is a shit. He's treating your people atrociously and he's treating my people atrociously. I'm not going to allow this man to go on demoralizing the people of Ogilvy & Mather.

—David Ogilvy, *The Unpublished David Ogilvy*

Summary / Fourteen Quick Takes / People *Really* First

... "give people enriching, rewarding lives"

... "desperate to have each of their team members flourish"

... "how things can be arranged to help that individual experience success"

... "become more than they have ever been before, more than they have dreamed of being"

... "do those being served become healthier, wiser, freer, more autonomous"

... "give great service to staff"

... "customers will never be any happier than your employees"

... "first you must WOW the people who WOW the customer"

... "250,000 people, every one of whom gives a shit"

... "build a culture in which individuals have the means to truly thrive, to succeed, to be happy in their work, to feel fulfilled and growing"

... "employees are our first customers, our most important customers"

... "ladies and gentlemen serving ladies and gentlemen"

**. . . "focus was totally on the staff; they were the ones
we wanted to make happy"**

. . . "joy is the core belief of our workplace"

To Do: Please re-read (and then re-re-read) and ingest and discuss
20H the quotes in this section. They all in effect say the same thing:
Put People *Really* First.

The reason for 14 "same-sames"—there's nothing else like
it in this book—is to underscore the importance of the idea
and to suggest that a lot of very smart people / leaders are
true "extremists" about the Put-People-*Really*-First idea and
strategy. What's not included in detail in these quotes is that
the economic upshot of these PPRF / Put-People-*Really*-First
strategies is growth and profitability that invariably outpaces
that of their peers.

Suggested (Required?!) Reading: Knock-Your-Socks-Off-Success through Putting People Really First

"Hard evidence" (if you need it) from those who have
walked-the-talk on this crucial (nothing-but-nothing-is-more-
important) topic:

*Nice Companies Finish First: Why Cutthroat Management
Is Over—and Collaboration Is In*, by Peter Shankman with
Karen Kelly

*Uncontainable: How Passion, Commitment, and Conscious
Capitalism Business Where Everyone Thrives*, by Kip Tindell,
CEO Container Store

Firms of Endearment: How World-Class Companies Profit from Passion and Purpose, by Raj Sisodia, Jag Sheth, and David Wolfe

The Good Jobs Strategy: How the Smartest Companies Invest in Employees to Lower Costs and Boost Profits, by Zeynep Ton

Joy, Inc.: How We Built a Workplace People Love, by Richard Sheridan, CEO Menlo Innovations

Employees First, Customers Second: Turning Conventional Management Upside Down, by Vineet Nayar, CEO, HCL Technologies

The Customer Comes Second: Put Your People First and Watch 'Em Kick Butt, by Hal Rosenbluth, former CEO, Rosenbluth International

Patients Come Second: Leading Change by Changing the Way You Lead, by Paul Spiegelman and hospital CEO Britt Berrett

4.21

Putting People *Really* First / Part-Timers as Family

1998-2014: *Fortune* reported that just twelve enterprises had been on its "100 best companies to work for in the United States" list *every year*, for all 16 years of that list's existence. Along the way, among other things, the Super Twelve created 341,567 new jobs—that amounts to job growth of 172 percent (shareholder returns, for the publicly traded companies among the Super Twelve, also dramatically outpaced the market as a whole).

The Super Twelve:
Publix
Whole Foods
Wegmans
Nordstrom
Marriott
REI
Four Seasons
Cisco Systems
Goldman Sachs
SAS Institute
W.L. Gore
TDIndustries

Note: Over half (!), fully 7 / 12ths (the first seven on the list) of the "consistently best of the 100 best" are in so-called "necessarily low wage" components of the service industry.

Performance example:
Retail turnover in general . . . 65 percent;
Publix (groceries, one of the 7 / 12) turnover . . . five percent.

Relative to the 2016 version of the list, *Fortune* reported that the Super Twelve have . . . "only one thing in common. They take generous care of their part-timers."

To Do: "Take generous care of their part-timers":
21 And you???????????????????????????

4.22

People First / Why Is it Not Obvious to All:

"Coach Belichick, Your Players Are Very Important"

Tom Peters, the high-profile business consultant, is brought in by the New England Patriots to do a stem-to-stern franchise evaluation. The day has arrived for the presentation. Peters, dressed McKinsey style that he knows so well (conservative dark suit with understated tie), begins, earnestly, "Coach Belichick, after a several month analysis, my colleagues and I have reached the conclusion that your players are very important to the franchise." At that point, Mr. Belichick, who doesn't know whether to laugh or cry, picks up one of the several Super Bowl trophies on his desk, throws it at Mr. Peters, and chases him to the door.

The deflated Mr. Peters had felt comfortable with the value of his "players-are-important" / "people first" assessment. That sort of finding would be a worth-the-fee revelation to many "hard-nosed" / "no nonsense" business clients. The marketing-trained hotel chief would have expected the issue to be segmentation strategy or marketing approach. The accounting-trained banker would have expected a diagnosis of "too much overhead" with an assessment of how many people can be tossed over the side. But Peters would instead say, "Sir, you have a demotivated, under-trained, under-rewarded staff, which is causing a big-league customer disconnect, puny innovation accomplishments, and half-assed implementation of most of your projects." That is, Peters would have surprised the hotel / banker Big Cheese with his "people are important" / "invest more in people" message.

People First / Belichick: "Do you think I'm an idiot, Mr. Peters?"
People First / Hotelier & Banker: Breakthrough idea!

(Yes, exaggeration, but, frankly, not by all that much based on my 40+ years of experience.)

My simple point, then:

The complete frontline staff complements in the hotel (from housekeeping to accounting), the six- or 60-person consultancy, the enterprise software firm, the nuts and bolts factory, the nuclear power plant . . . are precisely as important as are the players on Mr. Belichick's New England Patriots football team, the musicians in the 11-time National Champion Dartmouth High School Marching Band, and the 700 sailors who were in U.S. Naval Mobile Construction Battalion NINE, in which I served in Vietnam in 1966-67.

United States Navy.
People first.
Massachusetts General Hospital.
People first.
Four Seasons Hotel / Boston.

People first.
Dartmouth High School.
People first.
Google.
People first.
Apple.
People first.
San Francisco Forty-Niners.
People first.
Cornell Big Red lacrosse team.
People first.
Somerset Subaru.
People first.
Bayside Restaurant.
People first.
Dan Cook Lawn and Garden Service.
People first.

People first.
Damn it.
People first.
Damn it.

Damn it.
Damn it.
Damn it.

Okay????

To Do: **22**	Will "People First" be reflected in your activities in the next 30 minutes? People first. This morning? People first. This afternoon? People first. Today? People first. Tomorrow? People first. Forever. And ever . . .

4.23

DSCPHOSCPFGPMWLBB:

Department of Seriously Cool People Helping Other Seriously Cool People Flourish and Grow and Prosper and Make the World a Little Bit Better

Confession. I hate the term "HR.'" On the seventh of November 1942, my father entered the delivery room to get his first peek at me, newly arrived. My mother smiled up at my dad and said, (I was first born)

"Look, Frank, finally, our own little human resource."

I am Tom Peters. I am NOT a "human resource." You (reader) are Antoinette Banerjee, not a "human resource."

"HR" is . . . contemptible, disgusting, demeaning, and self-defeating. Label me and treat me like a "human resource," and I will reward you with mechanistic disengagement.

What's the alternative?

Simple: **DSCPHOSCPFGPMWLBB**

Department of Seriously Cool People Helping Other Seriously Cool People to Flourish and Grow and Prosper and Make the World a Little Bit Better

Okay? My extended Twitter Family gave this a hearty thumbs up, with a jillion retweets, several including door signs featuring DSCPHOSCPFGPMWLBB.

To Do: Action! Now! I am not a "human resource"! Pledge: I hereby
23 and forevermore banish the term "HR."

4.24

Evaluations: People Are *Not* "Standardized."

Evaluations Should *Not* Be Standardized. Ever.

Every team member plays a different role—ask any sports coach. Every team member is on a different rung of the development ladder. Every team member is dealing with her or his set of personal issues. The plea / demand here for non-standardization of evaluations applies to e-v-e-r-y-o-n-e, as much to Starbucks baristas and Hilton housekeepers as to corporate VPs and Golden State Warriors players and members of the San Francisco Ballet.

Some Evaluation Commandments:

Remember: You are not evaluating "members of your project team." You are evaluating Omar Khan, Janet Yarnell, Jose Salibi Neto . . . .

Effective evaluations emerge from a series of loosely structured, continuing conversations, not from filling out a form once every six months or year.

Boss: Does it take you at least a day to prepare for a one-hour evaluation conversation? If not, you are not serious about the meeting or the employee being evaluated.

Boss: If you are not exhausted after an evaluation conversation, then it wasn't a fully invested conversation.

This sub-section should be 10×longer. Our skill at giving feedback stinks in 9 out of 9.1 cases (9 out of 9.01?). There is a substantial literature around this topic that should be on your reading list. And more: Some superstar experts flatly say people don't need feedback; they need encouragement that vaults them to the next level. Consider:

"In over twenty-five years of experience in business, I've seen how detrimental constant feedback can be, how it chips away at our powers of discernment and self-confidence. . . . I've also seen what real conversations about the ways in which we approach problems or interact with our team can do, as long as they are genuine, nurture our unique essence and empower us to build our capacity, to reach further than we thought possible. In these kinds of conversations, you can't give precise advice for how to color inside the lines, or even offer support for not thinking outside the box—you must abandon the lines and the box in search of something completely unknown."

From the Foreword to *No More Feedback: Cultivate Consciousness at Work*, by Carol Sanford. *No More Feedback* is one of a kind, a genuinely original and profoundly important piece of extraordinarily well-researched work. Sanford begins the main body of the book like this, "I will admit from the start that this is a contrarian view of a subject that *I love to hate.* Feedback." (Her italics.)

4.25

Promotion Decisions / Life-or-Death

Promotions are "life-or-death decisions."

—Peter Drucker, *The Practice of Management*

Amen. "Life-or-death." And the implicit suggestion is that the promotion decision should be treated with the extreme care accorded to any strategic enterprise decision.

I have no doubt that you are "serious" about promotion decisions. I strongly suspect (am dead certain?) that you are not serious enough, especially promotion to frontline leadership slots (see section 1.4, frontline leaders as Corporate Strength #1).

Hard fact: Every promotion decision is a "CEO decision." That is, do you want Maria or Mark or Saul or Hana Mei to be "CEO / Purchasing Department" . . . for the next five years? (That's a B-I-G deal.)

To Do: 25A	Your next promotion decision has incredible strategic impact. Please (please!) treat it accordingly.
To Do: 25B	Do a quick review of section 1.4, the strategic importance of frontline chiefs. I can think of no decision of any sort that will be more important than your next promotion decision for an open frontline leader slot. Act accordingly!!!

4.26

People *Really* First / E-Cubed

Extreme Employee Engagement

EEE / Extreme Employee Engagement maximizes the quality of customer engagement.

EEE maximizes customer retention.

EEE turns "customers" into "fans."

EEE makes it safe to take risks and make mistakes, which in turn generates and maximizes innovation at all levels of the organization.

EEE underpins and spurs teamwork.

EEE reduces friction and enhances co-operation, which dramatically improves all-important cross-functional communication and innovation associated therewith.

EEE improves the quality of joint ventures.

EEE enhances co-operation and communication which in turn increases productivity and quality.

EEE dramatically improves execution.

EEE is the best defense against the AI tsunami—and by and large makes AI a partner / ally rather than enemy.

EEE spurs the humanism of everything—which is not readily copy-able by AI in the foreseeable future.

EEE reduces turnover and stabilizes the work force.

EEE makes it possible to recruit top talent.

EEE means top employees are far more likely to stay with the organization.

EEE improves the reputation of the company as viewed by all stakeholders.

EEE improves community relations.

EEE is a contribution to humanity.

EEE makes coming to work a pleasure—not a pain.

EEE makes it possible for leaders to look in the mirror and smile.

EEE is Competitive Advantage #1

EEE is the bedrock of Excellence. (No EEE, no Excellence. It's that simple.)

EEE (bean counters take note) is a peerless / the best sustainable profit-maximization tool.

EEE = $$$$ / Money (lots of) in the bank for one and all.

This is a looong list. But I firmly believe it does not amount to overstatement. Simply put, EEE has no peers when it comes to enterprise performance, getting ahead of the "AI tsunami" and doing the right thing for our team members and their communities, particularly in the midst of the crisis we now face.

To Do: 26 **"BOTTOM LINE":** On a 1-10 scale, how does your unit / organization / company score on EEE? (No hasty answer, please. Your "EEE Score" is arguably the most important number in your Professional Universe.)

4.27

Your Choice:
Artificial Intelligence.
Foe? Or Friend?

A ceaselessly cited 2015 Oxford University study, referred to earlier, predicteded that artificial intelligence would put 50 percent of American white collar jobs at risk in the course of the next two decades. Most experts say that estimate is too high—but none deny that the impact will be significant.

The position taken here is that we have a choice. AI need not be seen as mortal enemy. To the contrary. AI can abet, and abet significantly, the ideas offered in these pages. The best of the best—several of whom you will meet in this book—are bold technology investors, but they by and large use that technology to enhance human interaction, not replace it.

There is a descriptor for this: AI vs. IA. That is: AI / Autonomous (no humans) Intelligence versus IA / Intelligence Augmented (improved human performance).

AuraPortal, a Florida-based remote working and business productivity software company, describes Augmented Intelligence and the AI-IA tug-of-war nicely on its website:

"Artificial Intelligence . . . has the potential to disrupt practically all industries. But tech companies are beginning to think of AI in a different way as they understand that higher business value can be achieved by combining human and AI activities.

"Augmented Intelligence, also referred to as Intelligence Amplification (IA), cognitive augmentation, and enhanced intelligence, is in essence Artificial Intelligence with a twist. While Artificial Intelligence is the creation of machines to work and react like humans, Augmented Intelligence is using those same machines with a different approach—to enhance the human worker. Augmented Intelligence involves people and machines working together, each playing to their own strengths to achieve greater business value. In other words, the primary objective of IA is to empower humans to work better and smarter.

"Kjell Carlsson, senior analyst at Forrester, says Augmented Intelligence is the key to driving rapid business with AI. He explains, 'Companies that are making headway with Artificial Intelligence, that are driving new business value quickly and have results to show for it, are more often than not using AI technologies to make the life of an employee better.' He concludes, 'Augmented Intelligence is usually a better approach than using AI to replace human intelligence.'

"In recent years, in AI technology rankings in terms of the value they create, Augmented Intelligence was ranked in second place, just below virtual agents [a computer generated, animated, artificial intelligence virtual character that leads an intelligent conversation with users . . . .]. However, Gartner predicts that

AI augmentation will surpass all other types of AI initiatives," creeping into first place this year, then exploding as we reach 2025."

The people-centric business excellence that is the centerpiece and raison d'être of this book comes down heavily on the side of widely employing IA / Intelligence Augmented / Intelligence Amplification. And as described here, the IA-People (Really) First union is a winner for one and all, a boon to the employee and the basis for product and service differentiation that will significantly boost the financial performance.

To Do:
27

Do not run and hide when you hear the chant, "AI is coming around the bend." First, get smart. Techie or not, devote significant time to the study of AI / IA. This should be a personal priority. and it should be launched right now. Techie or not, junior or senior, small company or large, engage in group discussions which examine IA possibilities; these discussions should include customers and vendors. Also, regardless of your rank or area of specialty, make friends—good friends, I'd suggest—with people in the information systems group at your firm.

Repeat:
Get smart-er today.
Not tomorrow.

4.28

People First:
A Peerless Legacy

"In a way, the world is a great liar. It shows you it worships and admires money, but at the end of the day it doesn't.

It says it adores fame and celebrity, but it doesn't, not really.

The world admires, and wants to hold on to, and not lose, goodness. It admires virtue.

At the end it gives its greatest tributes to generosity, honesty, courage, mercy, talents well used, talents that, brought into the world, make it better. That's what it really admires. That's what we talk about in eulogies, because that's what's important.

We don't say, 'The thing about Joe was he was rich!' We say, if we can . . .

'The thing about Joe was he took good care of people.'"

—Peggy Noonan, "A Life's Lesson," on the life and legacy of journalist Tim Russert, *Wall Street Journal*

To Do:
28

The thing about _____ (your name) was . . .

(FYI: Multiply this 10× or 100× as we face COVID-19 and social unrest.)

5

Extreme Sustainability

5.29

Extreme Sustainability

Environmental Impact

Climate-Change Urgency

"Sustainability: It's the right thing to do, it's the smart thing to do, it's the profitable thing to do."
—Hunter Lovins

"Buy less, choose well, make it last. Quality rather than quantity: That is true sustainability. If people only bought beautiful things rather than rubbish, we wouldn't have climate change!"
—Vivienne Westwood

"What is clear is that many of our conventions and practices are no longer valid for the context in which we now find ourselves. . . . A multitude of social and environmental indicators make it only too apparent that contemporary production systems and consumption patterns are physically, ethically, and spiritually untenable. And so we must move forward into unknown territory and explore new approaches that are more environmentally benign and personally and socially enriching."
—Stuart Walker, *Sustainable by Design: Explorations in Theory and Practice*

Climate change, it is agreed by all but the cranks, is proceeding at a demonstrably exponential pace. New and unimpeachable evidence of short-term, let alone long-term, world-upending damage is accumulating, it seems, by the day.

Business is directly or indirectly responsible for the majority of our environmental degradation, and business, with or without governmental incentives, must be responsible for reversing the tide.

To Do: 29A Radical solutions are required by mid-day. And non-radical contributions reducing environmental impact can begin within the hour—in a 6-person purchasing department and a 9-person finance department and a 3-person business, let alone in a large organization taken as a whole.

To Do: 29B Regardless of enterprise or unit size, put sustainability on your practical day-to-day agenda. Make it your responsibility, for starters, to educate yourself and your teammates, if they are not already on board. You will not turn the tide, but you can be a conscious and active part of addressing this issue. Right now.

First steps:

1. Add sustainability to your Vision & Values Credo—or its equivalent, if you don't have a formal statement.

2. Make sustainability a discreet and visible and formal part of all strategic analyses.

3. Sustainability should be a part of all formal leader assessments.

Suggested Reading:

The Green to Gold Business Playbook: How to Implement Sustainability Practices for Bottom-Line Results in Every Business Function, by Daniel Esty and P.J. Simmons

Sustainable Excellence: The Future of Business in a Fast-Changing World, by Aron Cramer and Zachary Karabell

Green Giants: How Smart Companies Turn Sustainability into Billion-Dollar Businesses, by E. Freya Williams

Confessions of a Radical Industrialist: Profits, People, Purpose – Doing Business by Respecting the Earth, by Ray Anderson and Robin White

Sustainable by Design: Explorations in Theory and Practice, by Stuart Walker

Sustainable Business: Key Issues, by Helen Kopnina and John Blewitt

The Sustainable Design Book, by Rebecca Proctor

Aesthetic Sustainability: Product Design and Sustainable Usage, by Kristine Harper

Cradle to Cradle: Re-Making the Way We Make Things, by Michael Braungart and William McDonough

Elegant Simplicity: The Art of Living Well, by Satish Kumar

Value-Added Strategy #1:

Extreme Humanism: A Mirror as Big as a Band-Aid

"Design Is the Fundamental Soul of a Man-Made Creation"

"Only One Company Can Be the Cheapest. All Others Must Use Design"

Introduction:
Design / Extreme Humanism

From what deep recess of my mind did it spring? As is often the case, a book. Specifically, from *Financial Times* management columnist Chris Lorenz in 1987, *The Design Dimension: The New Competitive Weapon for Business*. For me, the insights were fresh. And I was soon captivated, captured and starting on my now 34-year Design Obsession. And obsession it is. Alas, I am an engineer's engineer and somewhat (or so) aesthetically challenged. But my "design appreciation score" is 11 on a scale of 1 to 10. That appreciation score has skyrocketed all the more in the last few years. I see aesthetic sensibility and emotionally engaging experiences as far and away, not "the best defense against", but "the best offense for" confronting— even mastering—the likes of the looming AI incursion.

Design by my lights is "humanism," pure and simple. In fact, the term I've taken a shine to is what I call "Extreme Humanism." And, perhaps most important of all, I believe Extreme Humanism applies equally to 6- and 6,000-person firms. I believe Extreme Humanism applies to purchasing departments and sales departments and accounting departments as much as to the product development team. You may not buy it, but I think a financial report can be as well designed as an item of designer clothing. A report that is understandable to someone whose math topped out in the fifth grade. Compelling. Straightforward. 100 percent jargon-free. Attractive (yes). Draws you in rather than sends you running. Et cetera.

Design / Extreme Humanism is . . . life.

Design / Extreme Humanism is . . . soul.

Design / Extreme Humanism . . . makes us smile.

Design / Extreme Humanism . . . makes our partners smile.

Design / Extreme Humanism . . . makes us proud.

Design / Extreme Humanism is . . . Marketplace Differentiator #1.

Design / Extreme Humanism is . . . "a tiny mirror about as big as a Band-Aid."

A Tiny Mirror About as Big as a Band-Aid.

"Janet Dugan, a healthcare architect, took inspiration from her recent experience having an MRI (Magnetic Resonance Image) scan. While she was lying still and waiting, she noticed a small mirror that had been placed below the head support piece. It was angled so that she could see through the barrel to the radiology technician and make eye contact with him. 'What a small thing,' she told me. 'And yet what a difference it made. I felt less alone. I was connected to another person at the very moment I needed support. And even though I'm not claustrophobic, it calmed me some to be able to see out of the barrel . . . I [saw] the technician was friendly and that the nurse went out of her way to make me laugh. . . . I firmly believe in the power of design to contribute to the healing process—architecture can shape events and transform lives. But that day, in that experience, the thing that really gave me comfort was a tiny mirror about as big as a Band-Aid."

—Tim Leberecht, *The Business Romantic: Give Everything, Quantify Nothing, and Create Something Greater Than Yourself*

6.30

Value-Added Strategy #1: Extreme Humanism / Design Primacy. Ubiquitous Design-Mindfulness.

Extreme Humanism / Design Primacy

The production of commodities, products and services, will, as time passes (and perhaps not much time), be largely performed by some combination of AI and robotics. Yet differentiation marked by human involvement is entirely possible. Albeit it will require a mindset that today is practiced by a relatively small share of enterprises.

That must change.

The new world (success) order is what I have labeled . . . "Extreme Humanism." That Extreme Humanism is best expressed through ubiquitous design-mindfulness, which can be practiced in *every* nook and *every* cranny of *every* organization.

Extreme Humanism: *"He said for him the craft of building a boat was like a religion. It wasn't enough to master the technical details of it. You had to give yourself up to it spiritually; you had to surrender yourself absolutely to it. When you were done and walked away, you had to feel that you had left a piece of yourself behind in it forever, a bit of your heart."*

—Daniel James Brown, on George Yeoman Pocock, premier racing shell designer and builder, in *The Boys in the Boat: Nine Americans and Their Epic Quest for Gold at the 1936 Berlin Olympics*

Extreme Humanism: *"Every business school in the world would flunk you if you came out with a business plan that said, 'Oh, by the way, we're going to design and fabricate our own screws at an exponentially higher cost than it would cost to buy them.' But these aren't just screws. Like the [Nest] thermometer itself, they're better screws, epic screws, screws with, dare I say it, deeper meaning. Functionally, they utilize a specific thread pattern that allows them to go into nearly any surface, from wood to plaster to thin sheet metal. And the [custom] screwdriver feels balanced to the hand. It has the Nest logo on it and looks 'Nest-y,' just like everything from Apple looks 'Apple-y.'"*

—Tony Fadell, founder of Nest, in *The Soft Edge: Where Great Companies Find Lasting Success,* by Rich Karlgaard

Design that Makes a Lasting Difference / Design that Sticks:
100 Percent About Deep Emotional Connection

"Having spent a century or more focused on other goals—solving manufacturing problems, lowering costs,

making goods and services widely available, increasing convenience—we are increasingly engaged in making our world special. More people in more aspects of life are drawing pleasure and meaning from the way their persons, places and things look and feel. Whenever we have the chance, we're adding sensory, emotional appeal to ordinary function."

—Virginia Postrel, *The Substance of Style: How the Rise of Aesthetic Value Is Remaking Commerce, Culture, and Consciousness*

Leader-as-Designer-Extreme-Humanist Connects Emotionally to the Product or Service and Those Who Develop It ("Epic Screws, Screws with Deeper Meaning").

Leader-as-Designer-Extreme-Humanist Connects Emotionally to the Larger Community.

Leader-as-Designer-Extreme-Humanist Connects Emotionally to Customers-Vendors.

Customers-Vendors Connect Emotionally to Leader-as-Designer-Extreme-Humanist.

My proposition is that every leader becomes a de facto designer and must be hired for or acquire a full-fledged design sensibility. In an organization truly permeated with Design Mindfulness / Extreme Humanism / Extreme Emotional Connection, "design sensibility" is as evident in a training course or social media campaign or approach to hotel housekeeping activities (remember those tucked in shower curtains—Conrad Hilton's Life Lesson #1) as in the product or service sold directly to the external-paying customer.

(Clarification: This is not to suggest that every leader must have a degree from RISD, Parsons, or the Stanford d.school. I am suggesting evidence of some degree of aesthetic sensibility [an accountant who carves duck decoys as a hobby or is a superb home chef will do] and this also magnifies my fervent plea for more liberal arts grads and less MBAs with finance or marketing majors.)

To Do: 30A Please think deeply about: "You had to give yourself up to it spiritually; you had to surrender yourself absolutely to it." "Epic screws with deeper meaning." In order to internalize the idea of Design Mindfulness / Extreme Humanism / Extreme Emotional Connection, the likes of "epic screws" must be seen not as a "clever turn of phrase," but as a deadly serious way in which designers, and every formal leader, view the world, the product or service, and the external or internal customer.

I call it "the second D-Day," August 10, 2011 (the first having been the Normandy landings on June 6, 1944). On August 10, 2011, Apple's market capitalization surpassed ExxonMobil's. The design-driven firm beat out the natural-resources-based firm and became the most valuable corporation in America. After that, say I, design could no more be seen as lightweight "nice to do," "prettification." Apple > ExxonMobil. Case closed.

This is the essence of sustainable differentiation. This way of thinking, and immersive living, may not come naturally to you. As an engineer / MBA, it didn't come naturally to me. But that must change. For me it was linking up with people such as Donald Norman after his books *The Design of Everyday Things* and *Emotional Design* appeared; then came the great good fortune of having my Palo Alto office practically next door to

IDEO founder David Kelley, who became a pal and design mentor and nudger.

I effectively threw myself in front of the "design train." My wife is a textile artist / tapestry weaver. I most certainly am not. But my appreciation and championing of Design Excellence / Emotional Design is sky high. And now I am recasting it, with even more emphasis—and, given the times, much more urgency—as Extreme Humanism.

To Do:
30B
Join me in the (exciting) (urgent) (difference making) Extreme Humanism Adventure—by hook or by crook. Our professional lives and those of our mates depend on it!

6.31

Extreme Humanism. Design as Soul. Design as Serving Humanity. Design as Who We Are.

"The peculiar grace of a Shaker chair is due to the fact that it was made by someone capable of believing that an angel might come and sit on it."

—Thomas Merton, from *Religion in Wood: A Book of Shaker Furniture* by Edward Deming Andrews and Faith Andrews

To Do: 31A   Can you apply this in your corner of the universe—for example, Purchasing, IS, a three-person local accountancy? My unequivocal answer: YES!

To Do: 31B   Discuss and don't leave the room until you translate "believing that an angel might come and sit on it" into your new product—or training course.

"Expose yourself to the best things humans have done and then try to bring those things into what you are doing."

—Steve Jobs in Steve Denning's "The Lost Interview: Steve Jobs Tells Us What Really Matters," *Forbes*

"In some way, by caring, we are actually serving humanity. People might think it's a stupid belief, but it's a goal—it's a contribution that we hope we can make, in some small way, to culture."

—Jony Ive, chief designer, Apple

"Steve and Jony [Ive] would discuss corners for hours and hours."

—Laurene Powell Jobs

"We don't have a good language to talk about this kind of thing. In most people's vocabularies, design means veneer. . . . But to me, nothing could be further from the meaning of design. Design is the fundamental soul of a man-made creation."

—Steve Jobs

"It is fair to say that almost no new vehicle in recent memory has provoked more smiles."

—Tony Swan, "Behind the Wheel," review of the MINI Cooper S; *New York Times*

"Design is treated like a religion at BMW."

—*Alex Taylor*, "BMW Takes Its Own Route," *Fortune*

"Starbucks had become operationally driven, about efficiency as opposed to the romance. We'd lost the soul of the company."

—Howard Schultz, in a *Financial Times* interview, on Starbucks' problems which caused Schultz to reclaim the CEO job

"Romance" and "soul" animate the entire organization in Design-driven / Extreme-Humanism-driven companies. And, as usual, my addenda: This holds for that nine-person training department or two-person consultancy as much as Starbucks or Apple or BMW.

"As a marketing executive, I view business as one of the greatest adventures of the human enterprise—if not the greatest. But I am not just a businessman: I am also an unapologetic romantic. I believe the world would be a better place if we had more romance in our lives.
I believe that emotion eats reason for breakfast.
I am not a daydreamer, idealist, or social activist.
I am a business romantic."

—Tim Leberecht, former marketing chief, Frog Design, *The Business Romantic: Give Everything, Quantify Nothing, and Create Something Greater Than Yourself*

To Do:
31C

Consider / Reflect: "Greatest adventures of the human enterprise" / "unapologetic romantic" / "business romantic" / "emotion eats reason for breakfast." None of these phrases are "over the top" as I see it. All are consistent with the idea of "extreme humanism," which I—to repeat—see as "Differentiator #1" in the "age of AI." I would also suggest, perhaps an extreme view, that these design ideas are especially fit for this horrid time of COVID-19. Great design, as I have repeatedly emphasized, is about caring—and an organization devoted to caring, leaving the emotionless "lowest cost and least people" services and products behind and devoting ourselves to producing products and services that enrich people's lives.

Extreme Humanism: Lovemarks

"Shareholders very seldom love the brands they have invested in. And the last thing they want is an intimate relationship. They figure this could warp their judgment. They want measurability, increasing returns (always), and no surprises (ever). No wonder so many brands lost the emotional thread that had led them to their extraordinary success and turned them instead into metric-munchers of the lowest kind.

"Watch for the sign: Heads, not hearts, at work here. . . .

"When I first suggested that Love was the way to transform business, grown CEOs blushed and slid down behind annual accounts. But I kept at them. I knew it was Love that was missing. I knew that Love was the only way to ante up the emotional temperature and create the new kinds of relationships brands needed. I knew that Love was the only way business could respond to the rapid shift in control to consumers."

—Kevin Roberts, former CEO, Saatchi & Saatchi, *Lovemarks: The Future Beyond Brands*

Extreme Humanism / Design Mindfulness

Manifestations Throughout the Organization

"Seeking Business Romantic to Join Our Team"

From *The Business Romantic: Give Everything, Quantify Nothing, and Create Something Greater Than Yourself* by Tim Leberecht:

"Seeking Business Romantic to join our team: Reporting to the CEO, the Business Romantic will help colleagues, customers, partners, and society at large see the beauty of the business world with fresh eyes. Embracing hope as a strategy, the Business Romantic presents cohesive narratives that make sense of ever more complex and fragmented workplace and market conversations. Instead of focusing on assets and return-on-investment, the Business Romantic exposes the hidden treasures of business and delivers return-on-community. The

Business Romantic develops, designs, and implements 'acts of significance' that restore nostalgic trust in business as the most impactful human enterprise and provide internal and external audiences with brand and workplace experiences rich with meaning, delight, and fun. We're looking for a self-starter with strong entrepreneurial drive, exquisite taste, and a proven track record of managing the immeasurable. Specific responsibilities will include but are not limited to . . ."

To Do: 31D This was an actual job posting that got an overwhelming response. How about your organization? *Ready for a Business Romantic?*

Among other things, the importance and urgency of the umbrella idea should translate directly into, say, hiring practices. That is, to invade the entire enterprise with Design Mindfulness / Extreme Humanism appreciation, we need to pepper every nook and cranny with those who have the appropriate background and experience. No, I'm not suggesting a Design School graduate must necessarily be a full-time member of the People Department or Finance Department. But I am suggesting—very directly—that as we seek candidates for that People Department, Finance Department slot, we lean toward, say, Fine Arts majors or Theater majors or CVs that reflect an abiding interest in the arts. You want enterprise-wide Design Mindfulness? Hire throughout the organization those with appropriately demonstrated sensibilities / dispositions on their CVs. (This notion goes double or more with promotion decisions, again, throughout the entire enterprise.)

To Do: 31E Hire for an aesthetic disposition in all departments. Formalize the criteria.

Extreme Humanism /
Design Mindfulness
Believing That an Angel Might
Come and Sit on It

These are some of the compelling bits of the material we have just examined:

"Leave a bit of your heart behind"

"Epic screws, screws with deeper meaning"

"Believing that an angel might come and sit on it"

"Discuss corners for hours upon hours"

"Serve humanity by caring"

"Bring the best things humans have done into what you are doing"

"Provoke more smiles"

"Religion"

"Romance"

"Fundamental soul"

Emotion > Reason

"Seeking a Business Romantic"

"Create something greater than yourself"

"Lovemarks"

"Love is the only way to respond to the rapid shift in control to consumers"

To Do:	Please reflect.
31F	

Design Mindfulness / Extreme Humanism

Design Ubiquity / Design Is Your Next Four-Line Email

*"Design is everything.
Everything is design.
We are all designers."*

—Richard Farson, *The Power of Design: A Force for Transforming Everything*

"Typically, design is a vertical stripe in the chain of events in a product's delivery. [At Apple, it's] a long, horizontal stripe, where design is part of every conversation."

—Robert Brunner, former Apple design chief, in Ian Parker's "The Shape of Things to Come," *New Yorker*

Design is instinctively part of every decision—and, for that matter, every conversation. Tall order! But, to repeat myself for umpteenth time (it matters that much to me), there is little doubt that Design Mindfulness / Extreme Humanism-in-all-we-do is Differentiator #1 in the years to come. *For any and all organizations.*

Design Is:

The reception area.
The restrooms (!!!).
Dialogues at the call center.
Every business process "map."
E-v-e-r-y email and e-message.
Every meeting agenda / setting / etc.
The first five minutes after you enter the office / the first three minutes of a WFH / Zoom meeting.
Every customer contact.
A consideration in every promotion decision.
The ubiquitous presence of an "aesthetic sensibility."
This morning's MBWA / (Managing By Wandering Around) or MBZA / (Managing By Zooming Around).
A concern with the value of our products and services
to humanity.
And more.

To Do:
31G
Do you and your colleagues buy into this encompassing view of design with oomph? (Please discuss at length.)

6.32

Design / Excellence / Extreme Humanism / The Last Words: Not Cleanliness Alone, but the Beautiful and the Natural Also

"Rikyu was watching his son Sho-an as he swept and watered the garden path. 'Not clean enough,' said Rikyu, when Sho-an had finished his task, and bade him try again. After a weary hour, the son turned to Rikyu: 'Father, there is nothing more to be done. The steps have been washed for the third time, the stone planters and the trees are well sprinkled with water, moss and lichens are shining with a fresh verdure; not a twig, not a leaf have I left on the ground.' 'Young fool,' chided the tea-master, 'that is not the way a garden path should be swept.' Saying this, Rikyu stepped into the garden, shook a tree and scattered over the garden gold and crimson leaves, scraps of the brocade of autumn! What Rikyu demanded was not cleanliness alone, but the beautiful and the natural also."

—Kakuzō Okakura, *The Book of Tea*

"Meaning, Intuition, Silence, Reflection, Localization, Harmony, and Time"

"If design is to make substantial contribution to contemporary culture, it has to move beyond instrumental solutions to what are often rather trivial problems. From furniture design to household goods, from electronics to services, design's conventional but slender aspiration of creating 'delight' and 'pleasure' in the use of worldly things offers us little more than interminable novelty. . . . Design has to reach beyond such devices of desire that disable and disconnect us from each other and the world itself. . . . Today, design needs to address quite different questions . . . about priorities, values and meaning. To search for answers, we must look to the world of real encounters and lived experiences. . . . Design is concerned with meaning, intuition, silence, reflection, localization, harmony, and time."

—Stuart Walker, *Design for Life: Creating Meaning in a Distracted World*

"Only one company can be the cheapest. All others must use design."

—Rodney Fitch, *Fitch on Retail Design*

Extreme Humanism: Getting Started

Emotional Design / Extreme Humanism / Romance et al. are indeed crucial ideas. Try this reading list . . .

Emotional Design: Why We Love (or Hate) Everyday Things, by Donald Norman

Enchantment: The Art of Changing Hearts, Minds, and Actions, by Guy Kawasaki

Lovemarks: The Future Beyond Brands, by Kevin Roberts

The Business Romantic: Give Everything, Quantify Nothing, and Create Something Greater Than Yourself, by Tim Leberecht

Design for Life: Creating Meaning in a Distracted World, by Stuart Walker

To Do: 32A   No topic in this book requires more reflection. *Period*.

What's Left For Us Is Us

I talk a lot about EQ / empathy, about Extreme Humanism, Extreme Employee Engagement. Organizations are traditionally built on logic. B-schools preach logic. Well, AI is going to more or less usurp all that. "What's left" for us is us. To be more human, to gravitate to the "soft stuff".

Extreme Times / Domain Names Fit For 2021

ExtremeHumanism.com
ExtremeSustainability.com
ExtremeCommunityEngagement.com
ExtremeEmployeeEngagement.com
ExtremeDesignMindfulness.com
RadicalPersonalDevelopment.com
HumanismOffensive.com
FerociousListening.com
AggressiveListening.com

To Do:
32B

I yearn to convert each of these URLs into a full-fledged movement. Vounteers wanted! (I also, of course, yearn for these items to play the lead role in daily organizational life— and, quixotic as the quest may be, to see these concerns at the *top* of MBA curricula.)

Value-Added Strategy #2:

TGRs
Things Gone Right

Emotionally Engaging Experiences

Experiences That Stick

Small > Big

America's Best Restroom

7.33

Value-Added Strategy #2:
An Avalanche of TGRs /
Things Gone Right

Small > Big

The Yawning 8-80 Chasm

Customers describing their service experience
as "superior": **8%**

Companies describing the service experience they
provide as "superior": **80%**

—Bain & Company survey of 362 companies

TGRs / Things Gone Right
to the Rescue

A big part of closing what I call the "8-80 gap / chasm" (and it
is a chasm) comes via a truckload of TGRs-added. And added
and added.

Historically, "TG<u>W</u>s" / Things Gone Wrong was a premier quality measure—especially in the auto industry. Quality is still of the utmost importance, but the fact is that most things work pretty well—a low TGW score is imperative, but no longer the powerhouse differentiator it once was. Hence, I am suggesting a flip to the positive side of the equation, the numerator if you will: Distinction via special touches that I label TGRs / Things Gone *Right*.

TGR-ing is my choice, along with a heavy dose of Design Mindfulness as previously discussed, as the top drivers of distinction-2021-that-sticks. My flavor, though strategic in impact, is largely tactical—tweaking and tweaking and polishing and polishing our service, in particular, and product offerings—creating "delight" and "fans" and "can't-live-without-us" customer impact. And, of the utmost importance, with every member of the company contributing. TGR-ing is an "all hands on deck" "forever-and-ever" affair!

To Do: 33A   Formally or informally determine if you suffer from your own "8-80 Chasm." In bigger firms, this could be expensive and time-consuming. But worth it. Even in a tiny outfit, I'd suggest some sort of quantified measurement. And as usual in these pages, I insist that this applies exactly as much to internal departments as to customer-facing units. (We're all in "customer-facing units," right? Some, external customers, some internal customers—and customer means customer, with all that implies.)

To Do: 33B   Assessment in hand, think on, and then act on, some flavor of a vibrant, everyone-involved TGR-ing culture. Start time: TODAY. Finish time: NEVER.

7.34

Be the Best. It's the Only Marketplace that's Not Crowded.

Jungle Jim's / TGR Central. America's Best Restroom.

George Whalin's *Retail Superstars: Inside the 25 Best Independent Stores in America* is a masterpiece. Twenty-five peerless / imaginative case studies of mega-differentiators, independents who took on—and trounced—the Big Box crowd; and, to date, Amazon. Each and every one produces and directs its version of . . . "THE GREATEST SHOW ON EARTH."

E.g:

Shoppertainment Jungle Jim's* International Market, Fairfield, Ohio

(*Founder Jim Bonaminio is only to be called "Jungle"!)

From *Retail Superstars*:

"An Adventure in Shoppertainment . . . a 300,000 square foot store with 150,000 food products from 75 countries, and 50,000 visitors a week from around the world."

Jungle Jim's = TGR Central / a jillion "small" (or sometimes not so small!) differentiators:

"A seven-foot-high mechanized lion entertains shoppers by singing Elvis Presley's 'Jailhouse Rock.' . . .

"The Sherwood Forest display in English Foods comes complete with a talking Robin Hood. . . .

"An antique Boar's Head truck hangs above the Deli.

"A full-size rickshaw sits in Chinese Foods. . . .

"An Amish horse-drawn buggy in Meats . . .

"An antique fire engine atop the hot-sauce display [there are 1,400 sauce options . . .]

"Coney Island bumper cars filled with sweets in the Candy Department."

And at the tip top of the Jungle Jim's TGR list (per me):

"Two men's and women's Port-a-Potty situated in the front area of the store look as though they belong on a construction site rather than in a food store. But they are false fronts, and once through the doors, customers find themselves in beautifully appointed restrooms.

"These creative facilities were recognized in 2007 as 'AMERICA'S BEST RESTROOM' in the Sixth Annual competition sponsored by Cintas Corporation, a supplier of restroom cleaning and hygiene products."

Were I a retailer, there is no prize—of any sort, including the fabled Baldrige Award—I would rather win!!!

Whalin's apt assessment of the strategy of his twenty-five independent superstars:

To Do: 34

Let Jungle Jim's be a role model for you! That is, let your imagination run wild! Look for crazy TGR manifestations anywhere and everywhere—especially oddball places. Do not rest until you have "stolen" a "Crazy List" of at least twenty items. Get e-v-e-r-y-o-n-e involved!

Start: Today.
Repeat: Forever.

7.35

TGRs: Small > Big

TGR-ing: A Cultural Trait

"Courtesies of a small and trivial character are the ones which strike deepest in the grateful and appreciating heart."
—Henry Clay

This was the epigraph for my book, *The Little Big Things* and a life lodestar for me, launched by my 1977 "small wins" Ph.D. dissertation. Research demonstrated fact: The memories of the "trivial" "courtesies" (TGRs) can readily last a lifetime!

"Let's not forget that small emotions are the great captains of our lives."
—Vincent Van Gogh

And recall the epigraph for the opening EXCELLENCE section of this book:

"We don't remember the days, we remember the moments."
—Cesare Pavese, poet

"Small > Big"

—Henry Clay, Vincent van Gogh, Cesare Pavese, Tom Peters (yes, I've taken a little poetic license)

An "obsession-with-small" is a *culture* issue—i.e., an "all hands" environment where one and all are attuned to and obsessed with the little things that are collectively the most significant points of differentiation.

To Do: 35A   Small > Big is in fact a hard sell. We are hammered to achieve "breakthroughs" and "blockbuster strategies." So how do we turn an entire organization toward, yes, micro-TGR-mania???? (This, as I see it, is a must-do-now. Few things in these pages are more important.)

To Do: 35B   **Reading assignment:** *The Power of Small: Why Little Things Make All the Difference,* by Linda Kaplan Thaler and Robin Koval. *The Manager's Book of Decencies: How Small Gestures Build Great Companies,* by Steve Harrison, Adecco.

TGR / TGR-ing: A Cultural Trait

The Bedrock of Extreme Humanism

TGR-ing is not a one-off act. It is the product of an organization strategy and, especially, culture that vigorously encourages and supports 100 percent of staff "going the extra inch" to routinely—and without "permission"—invent and add touches that make an enormous cumulative difference. Which are arguably no less than the mainstay of Extreme Humanism.

A TGR-ing process supports staff spontaneity. "Hey, sure, try it."

A TGR-ing process features . . . continuous *applause*. That is, regularly publicly recognizing those who try the new thing, who go the extra inch.

TGR-ing is a deeply embedded way of life.

TGR-ing pays off Big Time on the bottom line.

Though each bit may be tiny, collective TGR-ing is . . . strategic.

To Do: Draw a picture of what a buzzing, blooming "TGR-ing
35C Organization" (your organization / tiny or giant) might look like. Take first steps?? (Repeat: This is a . . . very Big Deal.)

Value-Added Strategy #3:

Top-Line Focus

Better Before Cheaper

Revenue Before Cost

There Are No Other Rules

Value-Added Strategy #3:
Top-Line Focus

Better Before Cheaper

Revenue Before Cost

There Are No Other Rules

Take #1: From *The Three Rules: How Exceptional Companies Think*

1. "Better before cheaper.
2. Revenue before cost.
3. There are no other rules."

Deloitte consultants took a sample of 45 years of performance of 25,000 companies, and eventually winnowed the list to 27 superstars from which they extracted the three rules, which inspired the title of the book, co-authored by Michael Raynor and Mumtaz Ahmed.

TAKE #2: "Three Strategies to Dominate a Scary Economy" / Findings from the superior performers:

"They manage for Value [that's long-term value, not for short-term earnings]."

"They get radically Customer-Centric."

"They keep Developing Human Capital."

—Geoff Colvin, *Fortune*

All too often, especially among the big, Fortune 500-ish firms wedded to short-term shareholder value maximization, cost slashing and attendant body dumping are the preferred "strategic" tactics. But in the two extensive and trustworthy analyses reviewed here, revenue building through product / service Excellence took the gold.

9

Value-Added Strategy #4:

There Need Be No Such Thing as a Commodity

Garage as Cultural Icon

Plumber as Artist

9.37

Value-Added Strategy #4: There Need Be No Such Thing as a Commodity

Garage as Cultural Icon

Plumber as Artist

Parking Garage Excellence: "Carcitecture"

Derived from Bill Taylor's (superb) *Simply Brilliant: How Great Organizations Do Ordinary Things in Extraordinary Ways*:

1111 Lincoln Road.

That address has become a Miami Beach landmark. For example, when LeBron James, then with the Miami Heat and the world's best basketball player, introduced his 11th Nike shoe, he celebrated with hoopla of the first order at . . . 1111 Lincoln Road.

So just what is this special address?

A 300-car parking garage!

Developer Robert Wennett wanted to "re-interpret the original vision of Lincoln Road, set back in 1910." Among many other things, that meant having a makeover designed by the world-renowned Swiss architects Herzog & de Meuron. The "product" amounted to, per one member of the press, "carcitecture," an "unimaginable marriage of high-end architecture and car storage."

1111 Lincoln features, among many other things, public art and a grand staircase (joggers by the score work out there every morning—many then move onto in-garage yoga classes). Wennett calls it a "curated space which provides an experience, telling a story."

Wennett himself has lived in a penthouse at the top of the garage.

Is this "over the top"? Of course! But it is also a very profitable venture, a community-changer, and a peerless act of imagination!

Parking-garage-as-commodity?
Sez who . . .

Parking garage EXCELLENCE? Why not?
Parking garage EXTREME HUMANISM? Why not?
Parking garage TGR-HEAVEN-ON-MIAMI-EARTH? Why not?

Simply Brilliant features a bushel of such inspiring / unlikely superstar SME examples.

Value-Added / Excellence / The Local Plumber

The local plumber (or electrician or painter or . . .) does not provide a "commodity service" . . .

- **if** she knows her job cold

- **if** she is an obsessive student, habitually learning new tricks

- **if** she has a winning disposition (VBG / Very Big Deal)

- **if** she shows up on time on the dot

- **if** she is neatly dressed

- **if** she has a spanking clean (even in mid-slushy-winter) spiffy truck

- **if** she fixes the problem in an elegant and timely fashion— and clearly explains what was done and why it was done this way or that

- **if** she cleans up so that after the fact the client could "eat off the jobsite floor"

- **if** she volunteers to do a few tiny tasks outside the one at hand—gratis

- **if** she calls ("call" = phone, not email) 24 hours later to make sure all is well

- **if**, perhaps, she creates a blog with occasional posts featuring practical tips for her clientele; for example, a tiny Virginia swimming pool company became a literal "best-in-world" following such a social-media strategy (see below)

- **if** etc., etc. . . . .

She ain't a commodity!!!

I call such de-commoditization and the relentless pursuit of excellence . . . EDWPF / Extreme Distinction Worth Paying For! (And also, from the last chapter: TGR-ing on steroids.)

This is also at the heart of mid- to long-term job creation. Our value-adding plumber-electrician watches demand soar via word-of-mouth singing of her praises. Next thing you know, the one-person show is a three-person show, then a six-person show. Not only new jobs, but good new jobs given our plumber-electrician's commitment to excellence and to constantly learning new tricks-of-the-trade. Next up is, say, partnering with the local Vo-Tech and turning "all this" into a full-fledged Community Improvement / Job Creation / Ain't a Commodity Effort. Etc.

To Do: 37   Noodle on these two examples—the parking garage and the local plumber. Wild-Crazy-Unimaginably-Cool-Differentiation can occur . . . *anywhere*. Look for Superduperstar two-person and six-person operations with Sky High Reputations. Join me—the *In Search of Excellence* guy, right—in a personal search for EXCELLENCE which will separate you from the crowd. (Bonus: It's a helluva lot of fun to be Best-In-Town-By-Far plumber-electrician-tailoring shop.)

10

Value-Added Strategy #5:

Services (of Every Conceivable Flavor) Added

"We Will do Anything for You"

Department as "Cost- Center" to Department as Value-Adding Superstar "Professional Service Firm"

10.38

Value-Added Strategy #5:
Services (of Every
Conceivable Flavor)
Added

"We Will do Anything
for You"

Department as "Cost-
Center" to Value-Adding
Superstar "Professional
Service Firm"

Aircraft Engine Makers Become Systems Logistics Masters

"Rolls-Royce now earns more from tasks such as managing clients' overall procurement strategies and maintaining aerospace engines it sells than it does from making them."

—*The Economist*, "To the Rescue: Britain's new champions are bean-counters and PowerPoint artists,"

uPs to uPS / United PARCEL Services to United PROBLEM SOLVERS

"Big Brown's New Bag: UPS Aims to Be the Traffic Manager for Corporate America"

—Headline, *Bloomberg Businessweek*

"It's all about solutions. We talk with customers about how to run better, stronger, cheaper supply chains. We have 1,000 engineers who work with customers . . ."

—Bob Stoffel, UPS executive, in an interview with *Fortune*

"United Problem Solvers" is service marked. UPS now thrives, not on tossing packages onto the back porch, but on running (often taking over) others' entire supply-chain systems.

To Do: 38A

To survive in today's ferocious and topsy-turvy marketplace, a firm / organizational unit of any flavor needs to spread its wings, to continuously seek out and find new ways to help its customers. Among other things, this calls for a state of ECI / Extreme Customer Intimacy. Simply put, starting today, direct your attention toward understanding your customer's business—and the customer's team, from top to bottom— better than the customer does! (Which takes a helluva lot of time and effort!) It is not "a good idea" to do so. It is a strategic life-and-death necessity.

Services Added

PSF-ing / "Cost-Centers" To Value-Adding Superstars Save Millions of Jobs

I am arrogant enough to believe that we could have saved a million jobs, if only people had listened to me. But it's still not too late—in fact, now is the last chance hour as the AI hurricane comes ashore.

One of my worst-selling books was:

The Professional Service Firm50: Fifty Ways to Transform Your "Department" into a Professional Service Firm Whose Trademarks Are Passion and Innovation

The unloved "PSF 50," as my colleagues and I called it, was one long plea to transform a "bureaucratic department-cost center," always on the verge of being outsourced, into an innovative, world-class, IP-rich Center-of-Excellence (a sparkling PSF) adding untold value to the parent firm.

Here's the way the story might unfold:

To Do: 38B

The purchasing department sub-unit focused on, for example, technology acquisition and is re-incarnated as "Technology Acquisition Inc." The fourteen-person sub-unit / "cost center" becomes a full-fledged Professional Service Firm embedded (at least for now) in that 50-person purchasing department in a $200M business unit in, perhaps, a $3B corporation. Our reincarnated "cost center," now Technology Acquisition Inc., recall, aims to be "best of breed." Not the best "department" in the division or firm, but the best-damn-tech purchasing-organization in, say, the entire industry!

Technology Acquisition Inc.'s "product" (services packages) would exude Excellence and "Wow"! (That's what the PSF book commanded.) Its "IP" would grow like topsy and achieve renown! Technology Acquisition, Inc. would add immense value to the corporation as a whole *and* pursue substantial outside work as well.

"Bottom line" (when the PSF book was written—and even more so today): A "department" / "cost center," ripe for outsourcing, becomes an invaluable part of the parent corporation's value proposition. (And, writ large, the jobs in that department stay where they are . . . at home. Perhaps some of those "million jobs that could have been saved," as I arrogantly suggested!)

Value-Added Strategy #6:

A Bold Social Media Strategy

The "20-5" Rule

One Tweet >
A Super Bowl Ad

You *Are* Your Social Media Strategy

11.39

Value-Added Strategy #6: A Bold Social Media Strategy

The "20-5" Rule

One Tweet > A Super Bowl Ad

You *Are* Your Social Media Strategy

#1: 20 Years Down the Drain in five Minutes

"What used to be 'word of mouth' is now 'word of mouse.' You are either creating brand ambassadors or brand terrorists. . . .

"The customer is in complete control of communication. . . .

"Customers expect information, answers, products, responses, and resolutions sooner than ASAP."

"It takes twenty years to build a reputation and five minutes to ruin it."

—Warren Buffett from Brad Tuttle's "Warren Buffett's Boring, Brilliant Wisdom," *Time*

#2: One Tweet > A Super Bowl Ad

"I would rather engage in a Twitter conversation with a single customer than see our company attempt to attract the attention of millions in a coveted Super Bowl commercial. Why? Because having people discuss your brand directly with you, actually connecting one-to-one, is far more valuable—not to mention far cheaper! . . . Consumers want to discuss what they like, the companies they support, the organizations and leaders they resent. They want a community. They want to be heard."

—Peter Aceto CEO, Tangerine, pioneering Canadian financial services company

One tweet > A Super Bowl ad. That's a mouthful. Read it twice. (FYI: unimpeachable source.)

#3: Tiny Virginia Company / Global Powerhouse

"Today, despite the fact that we're just a little swimming pool company in Virginia, we have the most trafficked swimming pool website in the world. Five years ago, if you'd asked me . . . what we do, the answer would have been simple, 'We build in-ground fiberglass swimming pools.' Now we say, 'We are the best teachers in the world on the subject of fiberglass swimming pools, and we also happen to build them.'"

—Marcus Sheridan, River Pools and Spas, in Jay Baer's *Youtility*

Note: Tiny company. Tiny town. World-beater. Message: A universal opportunity courtesy social media. Soooo . . .

#4: Social Media / Everyone Is "In the Brand"

Miles (And Miles) Beyond "Empowerment"

You *Are* Your Social Media Strategy

"The Seven Characteristics of the Social Employee

1. Engaged
2. Expects Integration of the Personal and Professional
3. Buys into the Brand's Story
4. Born Collaborator
5. Listens
6. Customer-Centric
7. Empowered Change Agent"

—Cheryl and Mark Burgess, *The Social Employee: How Great Companies Make Social Media Work*

Message: Social Media is an "all hands" affair. And the "bottom line"? You are your social media strategy—like it or not, it defines you. (And we ain't seen nothin' yet.)

To Do: 39A	Assign a "Boldness-Thoroughness Score" to your social media activities. Get to work today if that score is anything less than "WOW." (What and who is covered by this dictate? E-v-e-r-y-o-n-e.)
To Do: 39B	Needed: an executive team member whose focus is social media.

12

Value-Added Strategies #7 & #8:

Women Buy E-V-E-R-Y-T-H-I-N-G & Marketers (Still) Don't Get It

"Oldies" Have A-L-L the Money & Marketers (Still) Don't Get It

12.40

Value-Added Strategy #7: The Gigantic, $28 Trillion+ Underserved Women's Market

"Forget China, India and the Internet: Economic Growth Is Driven by Women."

—"The Importance of Sex," *The Economist*

"Women now drive the global economy. They control $20 trillion in consumer spending, and that figure could climb to $28 trillion [within five years]. . . . In aggregate, women represent a growth market bigger than China and India combined—more in fact than twice as big as China and India combined. . . ."

—Michael Silverstein and Kate Sayre, "The Female Economy," *Harvard Business Review*

My translation: W > 2× C+I = $28T. (Women's market is more than twice [2×] as big as China + India and has already added up to $28,000,000,000,000.)

*"Women are **the** majority market."*

—Fara Warner, *The Power of the Purse*

Women's Share of Purchases / USA

Home Furnishings . . . 94%
Vacations . . . 92%
Houses . . . 91%
Consumer Electronics . . . 51%
Cars . . . 68% (significantly influence buying decision . . . 90%)
All consumer purchases . . . 83%
Bank account, choice of provider . . . 89%
Household investment decisions . . . 67%
Small business loans / Small business startups . . . 70%
Health Care (all aspects of decision making) . . . 80%
Philanthropy (women give 156% more than men) decisions . . . 90%
—Various sources

AND: In the U.S., women hold over 50 percent of managerial positions overall, including over 50 percent of *purchasing officer positions*. Hence, women arguably also make the majority of *commercial* purchasing decisions.

Women Buy E-V-E-R-Y-T-H-I-N-G: Womenomics

Add it up:
Women: #1 consumer purchases.
Women: #1 commercial purchases.
= Women buy . . . *everything*
—Various sources

"One thing is certain: Women's rise to power, which is linked to the increase in wealth per capita, is happening in all domains and at all levels of society. . . . This is

just the beginning. The phenomenon will only grow as girls prove to be more successful than boys in the school system. For a number of observers, we have already entered the age of 'womenomics,' the economy as thought out and practiced by a woman."

—Aude Zieseniss de Thuin, Women's Forum for the Economy and Society, "Women Are Drivers of Global Growth," *Financial Times*

and . . . and . . . and . . .

"$22 Trillion in Assets Will Shift to Women by 2020"

—*TheStreet*, (2015: "$22 Trillion in Assets Will Shift to Women by 2020: Why Men Need to Watch Out." FYI: It happened on schedule.)

Related Reading

Marketing to Women: How to Increase Your Share of the World's Largest Market, by Marti Barletta

The Power of the Purse: How Smart Businesses Are Adapting to the World's Most Important Consumers—Women, by Fara Warner

Why She Buys: The New Strategy for Reaching the World's Most Powerful Consumers, by Bridget Brennan

What Women Want: The Global Marketplace Turns Female Friendly, by Paco Underhill

The Soccer Mom Myth: Today's Female Consumer, Who She Really Is, Why She Really Buys, by Michele Miller and Holly Buchanan

Invisible Women: Data Bias in a World Designed for Men, by Caroline Criado Perez

S-L-O-W D-O-W-N. This is a "huge deal." Do not rush to judgement. Using primarily outsiders, do a thorough assessment of your orientation toward the women's market. The assessors should primarily or exclusively be . . . *women*.

12.41

Mastering the Women's Market

Can You Pass the "Squint Test"?

One indicator of readiness to embrace this colossal women's market opportunity comes from conducting what I call a "Squint Test":

1. Look at a photograph of your exec team.
2. Squint.
3. Does the composition of the team look more or less like the composition of the market you aim to serve? For example, if women buy 70 percent of your goods and

services (consumer and / or commercial), does the squint reveal a heavily female-laden top team, at least 50 / 50? If not, why not?

There are numerous reasons to have a robust share of women in senior positions. Social justice is one. The fact that research consistently shows that women are better leaders is another (see To Do 1.5 on page 46). But in this instance, I am simply suggesting—for reasons of market awareness and growth and profitability—that, in my opinion, true gender balance (or senior leadership tipped toward women, i.e., greater than 50 percent), consistent with current or potential market realities, makes economic sense.

(FYI: There is a stadium full of research about men's misunderstanding of the women's market, from design to marketing to distribution. For example, men, with some exceptions, cannot effectively design for women's preferences. And I admit to enjoying the firestorm that is ignited when I say this in a speech.)

To Do: 41   Can you pass the Squint Test? No? Get to work—today—on attaining a passing grade. Move fast. No excuses. (What possible excuses could there be?).

Closing Note and Question

To Do #1.5 (page 46): Women are the best leaders, negotiators, salespersons, investors. To Dos #40 and #41 (pages 179 and 182): Women buy . . . everything. In simple terms, is your organization aligned with those two sets of findings? Organization effectiveness and market performance and, dare I say it, Excellence depend on your answer to the question posed immediately above.

12.42

Value-Added Strategy #8: The Gigantic, Wildly Underserved "Oldies" Market

"Oldies" Have *All* the Money / How Could Marketers Be Soooo Clueless?

"'Age Power' will rule the 21st century, and we are woefully unprepared."

—Ken Dychtwald, Age Power: How the 21st Century Will Be Ruled by the New Old

"The New Customer Majority, age 44–65, is the only adult market with realistic prospects for significant sales growth in dozens of product lines for thousands of companies."

—David Wolfe and Robert Snyder, Ageless Marketing: Strategies for Reaching the Hearts and Minds of the New Customer Majority

50@50

"People turning 50 today have half their adult lives ahead of them."

—Bill Novelli, former CEO of AARP, 50+: *Igniting a Revolution to Reinvent America*

E.g . . .

"The average American household buys thirteen new cars in a lifetime, seven of them after the head of the household turns 50."

—Bill Novelli, 50+: *Igniting a Revolution to Reinvent America*

This was "one of those" stats that brought a lot into focus in a few words: *only-halfway-through-at-50.* (Marketers—you dolts [sorry]—listen-the-hell-up.)

"Households headed by someone 40 or older enjoy 91% of our population's net worth. . . . The mature market is the dominant market in the U.S. economy, making the majority of expenditures in virtually every category."

—Carol Morgan and Doran Levy, *Marketing to the Mindset of Boomers and Their Elders*

55–64 vs. 25–34:

New cars and trucks: 20% more spending by 55–64s than by 25–34s
Meals at full-service restaurants: +29%
Airfare: +38%
Sports equipment: +58%
Motorized recreational vehicles: +103%
Wine: +113%

Maintenance, repairs and home insurance: +127%

Vacation homes: +258%

Housekeeping and yard services: +250%

—Marti Barletta, *PrimeTime Women*

"Fifty-four years of age has been the highest cutoff point for any marketing initiative I've ever been involved in. Which is pretty weird when you consider age 50 is right about when people who have worked all their lives start to have some money to spend. And the time to spend it. . . .

"Older people have an image problem. As a culture, we're conditioned toward youth. . . . When we think of youth, we think 'energetic and colorful;' when we think of middle age or 'mature,' we think 'tired and washed out.' and when we think of 'old' or 'senior,' we think either 'exhausted and gray' or, more likely, we just don't think. The financial numbers are absolutely inarguable—the Mature Market has the money. Yet advertisers remain astonishingly indifferent to them."

—Marti Barletta, *PrimeTime Women*

"Marketers' attempts at reaching those over 50 have been miserably unsuccessful. No market's motivations and needs are so poorly understood."

—Peter Francese, publisher, *American Demographics* in a 1992 speech

(Please re-read!)

"Oldies don't 'have the money.' We have ALL the money."

—Tom Peters

FYI: "Oldies have all the money" is barely an exaggeration:

1. We have (more or less) all the money.
2. We have lots of time left to spend it.
3. And, by and large, the mortgage and tuition bills have been paid.
4. We have the Holy Grail: discretionary income.

To Do: 42A This analysis is hopelessly incomplete. For example, so just what is effective product development and marketing to oldies? For one thing, recall the comment in the prior section about men not being able to design for women. Relative to this section: ditto! By and large, "Youngies" cannot design effectively for "Oldies." Nor market effectively to Oldies. Etc. Simply put, to take advantage of this enormous opportunity arguably requires strategic realignment of the enterprise— from top to bottom.

To Do: 42B Relative to age and representation, apply the "squint test" discussed in To Do #41 to your marketing and product development group—this time the litmus test is age.

12.43

Last Words: Value-Added Strategies #7 & #8

Missed Mega-Opportunities

Gross Strategic Stupidity*

(*Strong Word . . . Carefully Chosen)

Recent (2019) research revealed that men are wildly over-represented in financial services leadership positions. And yet women make the lion's share of financial decisions. *And* they are more successful investors than men.

Likewise, we talk ceaselessly about millennial trends and continue to effectively ignore the "oldies market," as I call it. For example, oldies buy 50 percent of goods and services, yet are the target of just 10 percent of marketing spending.

The enormity of these two market opportunities, which I have been studying and ranting about for 20 years—and the pitiful response by businesses in general—is one of life's greatest professional mysteries for me.

To Do: Re-read these two sections. If you buy in—how could you not?—
43A then what are you going to do *today* to launch the process of examining where you are and where you might get to. De facto put this topic on every agenda. Now.

To Do: Recall the "squint test." Now for the *real* "squint test." Look
43B at a picture of the executive team. The marketing team. The product development team. The people department team. The purchasing team. Do every one of these pictures look approximately like the market being served? For example: Women. Blacks. Hispanics. Oldies. Whites. Other. Give yourself, if you are in a senior position ("senior" meaning not just the CEO and COO, but at the least the top couple of layers of management), a year to make Strategic Change. Twelve months hence, a repeat Squint Test. With, one hopes, different, perhaps radically different, results. Note: This applies to a 25-person operation, even a 12-person operation, as much, or even more, than to the Big Guys.

(Arguably, this is not a "strategic priority." This is *the* strategic priority.)

12.44

Eight Value-Added Strategies Summary

Value-Added Strategy #1: Design Primacy / Extreme Humanism. Design as Soul. Design is Who We Are. A Mirror as Big as a Band-Aid.

Value-Added Strategy #2: TGRs / Things Gone Right. Emotionally Engaging Experiences. Experiences That Stick. Small > Big.

Value-Added Strategy #3: "Top-Line" Focus. Better Before Cheaper. Revenue Before Cost. There Are No Other Rules.

Value-Added Strategy #4: There Need Be No Such Thing as a Commodity. "Cultural Icon." Plumber As Artist.

Value-Added Strategy #5: Services Added. "We'll Do Anything and Everything For You."

Value-Added Strategy #6: A Bold Social Media Strategy / The "20-5" Rule. One Tweet > A Super Bowl Ad. You *Are* Your Social Media Strategy.

Value-Added Strategy #7: Women Buy *Everything*. The Gigantic ($28 Trillion+), Under-Served Women's Market.

Value-Added Strategy #8: Oldies Have *All* the Money. The Gigantic Wildly Underserved "Oldies" Market. (How Could Marketers Be So Clueless?)

13

Whoever Tries The Most Stuff (And Screws The Most Stuff Up The Fastest) Wins

Serious Play

The Essence of Innovation

Fail. Forward. Fast.

Diversity Trumps Ability

Learn Not to Be Careful

13.45

Innovation #1
WTTMSW / Whoever Tries
The Most Stuff Wins

WTTMSW is the alpha and the omega of innovation. To be sure, it seems simplistic, especially given the abiding importance of the topic of innovation today. My reply is that declaring WTTMSW-as-Innovation-Cornerstone-Centerpiece is the product of an enormous amount of thought and observation and hard study and experimentation over a span of four decades.

WTTMSW was de facto the lead point among the "Eight Basics" around which In Search of Excellence was organized. Point #1: "A Bias For Action."

We talk, appropriately, if excessively, about "disruption." Surely that means "blow up the business" actions? Perhaps, but my take is that the premier way to deal with disruption is a staff of 100 percent (100 percent = 100 percent!) full-fledged no-baloney innovators who are committed to the WTTMSW Dogma on a daily basis. (See the discussion below on "serious play.")

WTTMSW / R.F.A.

"Ready. Fire. Aim."

—Ross Perot, founder of Electronic Data Systems, on his pioneering, wildly successful approach to business. (Perot sold EDS to GM. He subsequently said EDS lived by "Ready. Fire. Aim." GM lived by "Ready. Aim. Aim. Aim. . . .")

WTTMSW / Strategy at Southwest Airlines

"We have a 'strategy' at Southwest. It's called 'doing things.'"

—Herb Kelleher, founder, Southwest Airlines

God bless you, Herb. The late Mr. Kelleher was a good friend; "walked the talk" is gross understatement!

WTTMSW / Bloomberg

"We made mistakes, of course. Most of them were omissions we didn't think of when we initially wrote the software. We fixed them by doing it over and over, again and again. We do the same today. While our competitors are still sucking their thumbs trying to make the design perfect, we're already on prototype version #5. By the time our rivals are ready with wires and screws, we are on version #10. It gets back to planning versus acting: We act from day one; others plan how to plan—for months."

—Michael Bloomberg, *Bloomberg by Bloomberg*

WTTMSW / Just Make Stuff

"I want to be a Photographer.
Take a ton of photos. Start a photo blog.
Organize an art show for your best work.
MAKE STUFF.

"I want to be a Writer.
Write a ton of pieces. Establish a voice on social media.
Start a blog. Write guest posts for friends.
MAKE STUFF.

"Talk is cheap.
JUST MAKE STUFF."

—Reid Schilperoort, brand strategist, on *"the one piece of advice"* that has helped him overcome creative blocks

Again, I fear the charge of "simplistic." Again, I resist. Just shut up and get off your backside. Make stuff. Do something. Do anything. Now. Now = Now. (FYI: This is . . . personal. I have never had anything even bordering on a plan. Or a grand goal. I just keep moving, and "the big stuff" invents itself along the way!)

To Do: 45 This *idea* is simple. The *execution* is anything but simple. That is, WTTMSW is about an inclusive "try it / try something / try anything / try it now" attitude. It is about no less than a way of life. And a way of life that is messy and non-linear, the opposite of the common "by the book," "follow the plan," "get appropriate signoffs" standard.

The first issue for you is: Do you buy the WTTMSW-as-all-hands-do-it-now-innovation-engine hypothesis? If you are inclined to do so, then draw a mental picture of an "all hands" / "try it" environment. What, for example, would it mean for you in your regular interactions in the course of a day? You (boss) and I have a virtual one-on-one exchange, and after a formal issue or two is disposed of, I ask *"What are you working on that's new and cool—and can I offer you a hand?"* That may sound a bit corny, which it is. But the point is to establish an expectation that everyone is constantly trying to add a twist or a turn or two twists and two turns to what they're doing. "Well, Max, you know that new weekly financial report we're working on. We're testing some new approaches to cutting the preparation time in half. For example . . ." And so on. Exchanges like that would occur naturally several times a day. And, again, all hands, every rank, every level of seniority, every department.

Stuff bubbling.
("Stuff" is the correct word. Something. Anything.)
All the time.
Everyone.
Everywhere.

13.46

Innovation

The Insanely Important Fast Failure Imperative

WTTMS (ASTMSUTF) W / Whoever Tries The Most Stuff (And Screws The Most Stuff Up The Fastest) Wins

"Fail faster. Succeed sooner."
—David Kelley, founder, IDEO

"Fail. Forward. Fast."
—High-tech CEO, Philadelphia

"Try again. Fail again. Fail better."
—Samuel Beckett

"Reward excellent failures. Punish mediocre successes."

—Australian exec to me at event in Sydney, stating "the six words that underpinned my success" (Definitely on my "Top 10 Quotes" list. And meant to be taken seriously / literally, i.e., "Reward. . . . Punish. . . .")

"In business, you reward people for taking risks. When it doesn't work out you promote them—because they were willing to try new things. If people tell me they skied all day and never fell down, I tell them to try a different mountain."

—Michael Bloomberg, *Bloomberg Businessweek*

"What really matters is that companies that don't continue to experiment—companies that don't embrace failure— eventually get in a desperate position, where the only thing they can do is make a 'Hail Mary' bet at the end."

—Jeff Bezos

"It is not enough to 'tolerate' failure—you must 'celebrate' failure."

—Richard Farson

Failures:

Reward!
Promote!
Embrace!
Celebrate!
The more the merrier!
The faster the better!

To Do: 46   Assuming buy-in on your part, discuss at length and over time with your colleagues, sticking to the strong language above (for example, *"embrace," "celebrate," "promote"*). Imagine steps to instilling a reward-failures-fast culture. This is hard work, as it is usually contrary to standard organization practice.

The leadership team must believe—head and heart and soul— in the power of fast failures. And that belief must be imbedded in the Corporate Culture. And must be "enforced" (reinforced) on, literally, a daily basis.

13.47

Innovation: A Cultural Mandate

All Hands Engagement in "Serious Play"

"You can't be a serious innovator unless and until you are ready, willing and able to seriously play. 'Serious Play' is not an oxymoron; it is the essence of innovation."
—Michael Schrage, *Serious Play*

Think carefully about the *idea* of "serious play." And a life of serious play. The issue—which is, in fact, a / the premier WTTMSW Requisite—is cultural: "How we live 24 / 7 around here?" I'd add that it is different from the likes of "continuous improvement" and "Agile." It is looser, more inclusive (again, 100 percent of employees), less regulated—it is, uh, . . . *serious play*. It is indeed worthy of an entire "must read" book by a superstar innovation thinker-researcher.

Want WTTMSW?

Precursor #1: An a-l-l-h-a-n-d-s-c-u-l-t-u-r-e-of-serious-play.

To Do: **Rack 'em up:**
47
1. WTTMSW / "MAKE STUFF"
2. Reward and Celebrate failures—the faster the better.
3. Serious play = Us.

13.48

Innovation: You Miss 100 Percent of the Shots You Never Take

"You miss 100 percent of the shots you never take."
—Wayne Gretzky

YES!!!!! Unequivocally on my "Top 5 Quotes" list. #1?

Innovation / WTTMSW / Even J.S. Bach!

"The difference between Bach and his forgotten peers isn't necessarily that he had a better ratio of hits to misses. The difference is that the mediocre might have a dozen ideas, while Bach, in his lifetime, created more than a thousand full-fledged musical compositions. A genius is a genius, psychologist Paul Simonton maintains, because he can put together such a staggering number of insights, ideas, theories, random observations, and unexpected connections that he almost inevitably ends up with something great. 'Quality,' Simonton writes, 'is a probabilistic function of quantity.'"

—Malcolm Gladwell, "Creation Myth," *The New Yorker*

Lesson: "Quality is a probabilistic function of quantity"
= WTTMSW.

Ponder it: WTTMSW / Even Bach. No hiding: This is deeply
"cultural." Hence implementation is hard, persistent work,
always a "work-in-progress."

13.49

Innovation #2
The "Hang-Out-With-Weird"
Strategy

"It is hardly possible to overrate the value of placing
human beings in contact with persons dis-similar to
themselves, and with modes of thought and action unlike
those with which they are familiar. Such communication
has always been, and is peculiarly in the present age, one
of the primary sources of progress."
—John Stuart Mill, 1806-1873, *Principles of Political Economy*

"The only real voyage consists not of seeking new landscapes, but in having new eyes; in seeing the universe through the eyes of another, one hundred others— in seeing the hundred universes that each of them sees."

—Marcel Proust, *The Prisoner*

The second of five Big Ideas in my take on innovation: Diversity. And diversity in the pure sense of the word—constant, planned exposure to significant differences on any and every dimension imaginable.

"You will become like the five people you associate with the most—this can be either a blessing or a curse."

—Billy Cox, sales training guru

"Great quote," you say. (I hope.) Fine: But please p-a-u-s-e-a-n-d-r-e-f-l-e-c-t. This is sooooo true, sooooo important. A first-order "strategic" issue. We all tend subconsciously (and if not consciously and constantly countered) toward "same-same." Which is a peculiarly bad, even disastrous, practice in the tumultuous years to come, the 21st century.

To Do: 49A	*P-l-e-a-s-e do a hard-nosed assessment of the diversity of those five people!*

We Are What We Eat. We Are Who We Hang Out With.

MANTRA: Hang out with "weird" and thou shalt become more weird. Hang out with "dull" / "same-same" and thou shalt become more dull. Period.

In madcap times, continuous contact with very different "others" is, yes, one more time, a *strategic* necessity—and it only happens as a byproduct of (1) thoughtful, (2) hard, (3) meticulous work. Alas, our default is indeed invariably "same-same."

"Who's the most interesting person you've met in the last 90 days? How do I get in touch with them?"
—Fred Smith, Founder, FedEx, query to me

Ouch: Fred asked me this as we sat in a Green Room awaiting a CNN interview. And I, supposedly on the leading edge, didn't have a good answer. A source of continuing embarrassment—25 years later.

To Do:
49B

And your answer is???

Diversity (Per Se) Trumps Ability

"Diverse groups of problem solvers—groups of people with diverse backgrounds—consistently outperformed groups of the best and the brightest. If I formed two groups, one random (and therefore diverse) and one consisting of the best individual performers, the first group almost always did better. . . . Diversity trumped ability."
—Scott Page, *The Difference: How the Power of Diversity Creates Better Groups, Firms, Schools, and Societies*

Read Scott Page's book.
Ingest.
This is "ye gads" powerful!
(To repeat: diversity per se trumped "the best and the brightest"!)

To Do:
49C

The conclusion presented here should inform virtually every gathering in the organization. My point: Be very very conscious of diversity when it comes to decision making!

Hang-Out-With-Weird / Next Steps

Pursuing diversity is . . . *strategic*. And enterprise-wide. It should be a major factor in, for example:

- Hiring decisions.
- Evaluations.
- Promotion decisions.
- Choice of vendors.
- Time management!!! (What is last week's "Weirdness score" based on a day-at-a-time assessment of your calendar?)
- Lunch-real or virtual. (220 working lunches a year. Does a listing of your last 10 lunchmates personify diversity / "hang out with weird"?)
- Meeting attendees. (Are "unexpected" people at any given meeting, representing divergent viewpoints?)

To Do: Do uncompromising diversity evaluations on these variables!
49D

The Bottleneck Is at the Top of the Bottle

"The bottleneck is at the top of the bottle. . . . Where are you likely to find people with the least diversity of experience, the largest investment in the past, and the greatest reverence for industry dogma? At the top."
—Gary Hamel, "Strategy as Revolution," *Harvard Business Review*

Oh so common.
Oh so true.
Oh so strategically costly.

Sample 10-Person Board of Directors Fit for 2021

At least two members under age 30. (Youth must be served / guide us at-the-top circa 2021. This is rare!)

At least four (or five? or six?) women. (Boards with female / male balance lead to very high relative hard-number performance. See To Do 1.5 on page 46.)

One IT / big data superstar. (Not an "IT representative," but a certified goddess or god from the likes of Salesforce or Google.)

One or two entrepreneurs and perhaps a VC. (The entrepreneurial bent must directly infiltrate the board.)

One person of stature with a "weird" background: artist, musician, shaman, etc. (We need regular, uncomfortable, oddball challenges.)

A certified "design guru." (Noteworthy design presence at board level is simply a must in my scheme of things!)

No more than one or two over 60. (Too many oldie boards!)

No more than three with MBAs*. (Why? The necessity of moving beyond the MBA-predictable-linear-analytic-overquantified-certified-vanilla model.)

—Inspired by Gary Hamel

(*Throughout this book, I have been merciless in my criticism of MBAs. Of course, I have one, from Stanford, no less. [I call myself a "recovering-engineer-MBA."] My gripe, which you have doubtless long since figured out, is that MBA programs, virtually without exception, focus on the "hard stuff" [which, of course, I call "soft"] and downplay the "soft stuff" [which I call truly "hard]. There are, of course, exceptions among MBA students. And also, of course, one of my singular goals is to assist MBAs in rebalancing in the direction of, to point out the title of this book . . . Extreme Humanism. I'd finally add that my AWOL "people-stuff" critique applies without question to all the professional schools—business, engineering, and medicine in particular.)

To Do:
49E   How does your Board (or Advisory Group) stack up?

13.50

Innovation #3
The Power / The Necessity
of Discomfort

"I'm not comfortable unless I'm uncomfortable."
—Jay Chiat, advertising legend, founder of Chiat / Day

"You've got to learn not to be careful."

—Photographer Diane Arbus to her students

"If things seem under control, you're just not going fast enough."

—Mario Andretti, race car driver

"Do one thing every day that scares you."

—Mary Schmich, Pulitzer Prize–winning journalist

To Do: 50	Take Mary Schmich's command literally—and act upon it! And: Far easier said than done! (More generally, don't race by these quotes. Consider them hard-nosed guides to daily actions.)

13.51

Innovation #4
Avoid Moderation / The
Power of "Crazy"

"We are crazy. We should only do something when people say it is 'crazy.' If people say something is 'good,' it means someone else is already doing it."

—Hajime Mitarai, former CEO, Canon

Kevin Roberts' Credo

1. Ready. Fire! Aim.
2. If it ain't broke . . . Break it!
3. Hire crazies.
4. Ask dumb questions.
5. Pursue failure.
6. Lead, follow . . . or get out of the way!
7. Spread confusion.
8. Ditch your office.
9. Read odd stuff.
10. Avoid moderation!

—Kevin Roberts was CEO of Saatchi & Saatchi Worldwide from 1997–2016. (His book Lovemarks is on my "best business books ever" short list.)

"Every project we undertake starts with the same question: 'How can we do what has never been done before?'"

—Stuart Hornery in "The Company Without Limits," *Fast Company*

"Let us create such a building that future generations will take us for lunatics."

—15th century builders of Seville cathedral

"We are all agreed that your theory is crazy. The question which divides us is whether it is crazy enough to have a chance at being correct."

—Niels Bohr, to Wolfgang Pauli

"The reasonable man adapts himself to the world: The unreasonable one persists in trying to adapt the world to himself. Therefore, all progress depends upon the unreasonable man."

—George Bernard Shaw, *Man and Superman: The Revolutionists' Handbook.*

"There's no use trying,' said Alice. 'One cannot believe impossible things.' 'I daresay you haven't had much practice,' said the Queen. 'When I was your age, I always did it for half an hour a day. Why, sometimes I've believed as many as six impossible things before breakfast.'"

—Lewis Carroll

To Do: 51 Turn these quotes into de facto "Guidelines" relative, for example, to every project you are working on, large or tiny. For example, score every project on "Craziness" using a 1–10 scale. Worry if you do not have mostly 6-plus scores.

13.52

Innovation #5
A Cri de Coeur for
Creativity 2020+

A Birthright, Nurture it
and Keep it Alive

"Human creativity is the ultimate economic resource."
—Richard Florida

*"Every child is born an artist. The trick is to remain
an artist."*
—Pablo Picasso

*"How many artists are there in the room? Would you
please raise your hands. First Grade: En mass the
children leapt from their seats, arms waving. Every child
was an artist. Second Grade: About half the kids raised
their hands, shoulder high, no higher. The hands were
still. Third Grade: At best, 10 kids out of 30 would raise a
hand, tentatively, self-consciously. By the time I reached
Sixth Grade, no more than one or two kids raised their
hands, and then ever so slightly, betraying a fear of being
identified by the group as a 'closet artist.' The point is:*

Every school I visited was participating in the systematic suppression of creative genius."

—Gordon MacKenzie, *Orbiting the Giant Hairball: A Corporate Fool's Guide to Surviving with Grace*

"My wife and I went to a [kindergarten] parent-teacher conference and were informed that our budding refrigerator artist, Christopher, would be receiving a grade of Unsatisfactory in art. We were shocked. How could any child—let alone our child—receive a poor grade in art at such a young age? His teacher informed us that he had refused to color within the lines, which was a state requirement for demonstrating 'grade-level motor skills.'"

—Jordan Ayan, *AHA!: 10 Ways to Free Your Creative Spirit and Find Your Great Ideas*

"Thomas Stanley has not only found no correlation between success in school and an ability to accumulate wealth, he's actually found a negative correlation . . . 'It seems that school-related evaluations are poor predictors of economic success,' Stanley concluded. . . . What did predict success was a willingness to take risks. . . . Yet the success-failure standards of most schools penalized risk takers. . . . Most educational systems reward those who play it safe. As a result, those who do well in school find it hard to take risks later on."

—Richard Farson & Ralph Keyes, *Whoever Makes the Most Mistakes Wins*

Aargh . . .

To Do:
52A

Okay, "aargh" is not very operational. I therefore leave it to you to address this issue relative to the schools, in particular, with which you are directly or indirectly associated. Need I say, given the social and tech mega-change that is afoot, this is an issue of supreme and urgent importance.

To Do: 52B This certainly applies to schools over the long haul. But, damn it, also make sure that your professional world is a full-fledged Exemplar of Creativity—involving 100 percent of employees and contractors. And I'd urge you to make creativity—per se—part of hiring criteria for every job and for 100 percent of promotion decisions. (In the Age of AI: Creativity = Survival. Related: Recall the Extreme Humanism discussion.)

14

Leading with Compassion and Care

You Must Care
MBWA / Managing by Wandering Around
MBZA / Managing by Zooming Around
MBWA / MBZA: Leader Activity #1
Acknowledgement: The Most Powerful Word
I Am a Dispenser of Enthusiasm
Listening: Core Value #1
Kindness Is Free
Read. Read. Read.

The leadership section of this book is tactical, not strategic.
No "vision." No "authenticity." No "disruption." Just . . . "STUFF."
That is, twenty-some tactics guaranteed to work. "Guaranteed" is a boastful term, but each suggestion here has been demonstrated to work. Time and time . . . and time . . . again.

My goal is for you to play. That is, cherrypick ideas. Give one or two a try. Start, uhm, today! (All that said, the first To Do, #53, spells out the bedrock beneath every one of these leadership tactics: You must care.)

Over to you . . .

14.53

"Give-A-Shit-Ism."
You Must Care.

"The one piece of advice which will contribute to making you a better leader, will provide you with greater happiness, and will advance your career more than any other advice . . . and it doesn't call for a special personality or any certain chemistry . . . and anyone can do it, and it's this: You must care."

—General Melvin Zais, U.S. Army War College address to senior officers (I once gave the annual Forrestal Lecture at the U.S. Naval Academy—and handed out 4,000 copies on CDs of the Zais speech that featured this "must care" quote. I thought it was that important.)

Bedrock: All these leadership "guaranteed tactics" are gibberish and an utter and absolute waste of time unless the leader or would-be leader really (really! really! no baloney, no ifs-or-ands-or-buts!) gives-a-shit / cares about people.

Give-a-shit-ism = You must care = Sine qua non.

(Reminder: This is precisely what was implied [and de facto commanded] in our earlier discussions of hiring and promoting. You want give-a-shit-ism? Hire for it. You want give-a-shit-ism? Promote for it.)

14.54

MBWA / Managing By Wandering Around / The Guiding Light of *In Search of Excellence*

"A body can pretend to care, but they can't pretend to be there."

—Texas Bix Bender, *Don't Squat With Your Spurs On: A Cowboy's Guide to Life*

MBWA / Managing By Wandering Around
—courtesy of Hewlett-Packard

MBWA was the animating force for *In Search of Excellence*; that is, business leaders not absorbed by abstractions represented in a strategic plan or voluminous financials. But business leaders, instead, as real people, in the field, in intimate touch with the real work and those who perform that real work.

It was 1979. The research for what became *In Search of Excellence* was in its infancy. The working title was undistinguished, the McKinsey "Organization Effectiveness Project." My colleague Bob Waterman and I were interviewing folks here and there. On our list of potential candidates was our near neighbor (we were berthed in San Francisco) in Palo Alto, a feisty, still relatively youthful, innovative company called Hewlett-Packard.

We took the 25-mile trip to Palo Alto, and were soon seated in HP president John Young's "office" (a cramped 8×8 half-walled cubicle) amidst the engineering spaces. At some point early in the conversation, "MBWA" spilled out of Mr. Young's mouth. I think he was talking about the famous "HP Way" and said that the cornerstone was this (odd to us) thing labeled "MBWA."

Bob and I didn't know it then, but as of that utterance, everything changed in our professional lives.

Mr. Young's MBWA, as it seems half the world knows today, is of course Managing By Wandering Around. And it meant and means . . . Managing By Wandering Around. The deeper meaning: You can't lead from your office / cubicle or via messaging or emailing or PowerPoint-ing or spreadsheet-ing. You lead by fully humanized interaction. This book exists to "sell" extreme humanism including personalized virtual interaction. With your team members and outsiders as well. The long and short of it: heavy investment in emotional engagement gets things done.

At any rate, here I am, 40+ years later, still begging. Begging you to drop what you're doing right this minute—and do a half-hour of MBWA. (Or MBZA. See below.)

Okay?

To Do: Demand Daily / D-a-i-l-y MBWA = Effective Leader Activity #1.
54A

MBWA = Fun!!!
(Or Resign.)

Why do you do MBWA?
Because it's fun!
And if it's not . . .

To be sure, via MBWA you learn close-up what's really going on in the organization. But there's more, much more. It came to me like a flash during a beach walk in New Zealand, 35 years after *In Search of Excellence*, that you do MBWA because it's, yes, fun. It's a delight, or should be, to be out in the work spaces with the folks who are on your team who wrestle with day-to-day problems. It's fun to exchange stories. You learn important "stuff," certainly. But that's just five percent of the whole. The rest is about camaraderie in a human organization / community. I'm tough-minded about this ultra-"soft" activity: If in fact you don't deeply enjoy being around and intimately engaging with your folks; if you don't deeply enjoy chatting up the Distribution Center team at 1:00 a.m., I sincerely suggest that you find something else to do with your life. Sorry.

To Do:
54B

Enjoy yourself!
Hang out with your great gang!
Get to know them better!
Learn about their highs and lows!
And: Listen! Listen! Listen!
(And, seriously, if you get no pleasure from the unstructured "hanging out," think about your life's work and what you are doing right now. That's heavy duty, yes, but imperative.)

MBWA: Last Words
Twenty-Five Store Visits Each Week!

"I'm always stopping by our stores—at least 25 a week. I'm also in other places: Home Depot, Whole Foods, Crate & Barrel. I try to be a sponge to pick up as much as I can."

—Howard Schultz. Starbucks Founder / CEO, "Secrets of Greatness," *Fortune*

One cannot even imagine the tasks to be done—big and small—that confront Mr. Schultz every day. And yet, somehow, he visits those 25 stores each week. It is a peerless indicator of the lengths to which an effective leader can / will go to stay in direct touch with the action and his employees and customers.

14.55

MBWA Meets MBZA

Managing By Zooming Around Becomes the "New Normal"

Many people with much more experience than I will chime in on this topic. I suspect that within 18 months, Amazon's virtual book shelves will sport 25 (minimum) new volumes on the "Seven Steps to Knock-Your-Socks-Off WFH Effectiveness."

My pitch is short I leave it to you to create, say, "better meetings." My goal is to remind you that the essence of long-term effectiveness at anything is excellent relationships from hither, thither, and especially yon, and that the essence of innovation is chance interactions—and neither of those things come naturally in the World-of-MBZA / Managing By Zooming Around.

But don't stop trying! Iron law (damn it): Social chitchat is what makes us human. Invent your own virtual ways to get that done. The key: Experimentation! Frankly, none of us, at the time of my writing this, know what the hell we are doing. So . . . make it up as you go along.

(FYI: I have, since March 2020, given close to 50 Zoom podcasts or presentations. I am wholly convinced that you can, in Zoom-world, convey and achieve caring, thoughtfulness, and empathy almost as much as in F2F / face-to-face world. "Bottom line": you can still "make it personal"!)

A few points about Zoom-ish meetings:

Do not let the talkative ones—the extroverts—hog the show. By hook or by crook, bring everyone into the conversation.

Do *not not not* use some frigging Machiavellian software tool to measure and micro-manage the airtime of participants. Don't become a virtual Frederick Taylor (the time-and-motion guru). It's up to *you* to make it work.

The golden rule: *Always positive.* Rarely negative. (See below: positive reinforcement is 30× more powerful than negative reinforcement—30× in general, and another 10× in today's fraught environment.)

Reinforcing a major theme from about page one of this book: Hire for EQ. Promote for EQ. The so-called "soft skills," which are the real "hard skills," are far far more important when it comes to leading in WFH / MBZA settings.

In COVID-19 time . . . be, Ms. Boss, a good and caring human being. Do not "cut people slack." That's defense. Instead, realize there are stresses and strains on every attendee that are beyond your imagination. Act accordingly, with "kindness," not "tolerance."

An employee of Parks Canada sent a memo around to all its WFH employees in April, when COVID-19 concerns preoccupied all of us. A recipient shared it on Twitter. Here are the "rules" contained therein:

Working Remotely—COVID-19 Principles

1. You are not "working from home," you are "at your home, during a crisis, trying to work."

2. Your personal physical, mental, and emotional health is far more important than anything else right now.

3. You should not try to compensate for lost productivity by working longer hours.

4. You will be kind to yourself and not judge how you are coping based on how you see others coping.

5. You will be kind to others and not judge how they are coping based on how you are coping.

6. Your team's success will not be measured the same way it was when things were normal.

This sort of thoughtfulness exhibited in that memo is worth its literal and figurative weight in gold. I suggest, Ms. Leader, that you steal it!

To Do: 55 Do your best. Experiment! Experiment! Experiment! And take a page out of Parks Canada's book: Be kind. Be thoughtful. Be human. It's a good thing to do. And, frankly, it's great for long-term productivity—cared for employees are productive employees.

Re: Zooming, there is another MBZA device—*the phone*! It is arguably a far more intimate medium for checking in with Yvonne (or Tom!) than email / text / Zoom. A close friend says a phone call is "an intrusion." I disagree, vehemently. A five-minute call can easily expand to 15 or 20 minutes, during which all-important digressions are worth their weight in more than gold. You cover the planned topic, weird rumors, a customer screw-up, find out that Yvonne's dad is very ill, etc. In my experience, this is far less likely to occur zooming, and it sure as heck ain't the stuff of texts or emails.

Good luck!

14.56

Meetings = Leadership Opportunity #1

Meeting Excellence or Bust

(Fact: Most of your time = Meetings = Leadership Opportunity #1 = Excellence Opportunity #1. By definition!)

Meeting Excellence: Every meeting that does not stir the imagination *and* curiosity of attendees *and* increase bonding *and* co-operation *and* engagement *and* sense of worth *and* motivate rapid action *and* enhance enthusiasm is a permanently lost opportunity.

Yes, extreme language. But if "meetings-are–what-I-do" is more or less accurate, then the definition above is, I believe, unassailable. Albeit tough to consistently achieve.

Meetings Rules: Prepare. Prepare. (And Prepare. And Prepare.)

1. Prepare for a meeting / every meeting as if your professional life and legacy depended on it. It does! In no way is that an

exaggeration! (In my experience, meeting preparation by bosses is contemptibly low.)

2. *See #1.*

3. Listening time > Talking time.

4. Under no circumstance whatsoever, including a meeting with the boss' boss, may a boss be one micro-second late to a meeting. (Late = Disrespectful.)

5. A meeting is a *performance*. (Which has nothing to do with drums and bugles, but everything to do with the ambience which the leader carefully establishes and nurtures.)

6. "Meeting Excellence" is *not* an oxymoron. (Damn it!)

Note: WFH / Zoom-world throws an apparent spanner into the works. You are going to have learn-and-practice (and practice and practice) your way to Virtual Meeting Excellence. It will not happen overnight. But, and I have observed this, it can be done!

Do not judge yourself harshly for the unevenness of the learning process. We are developing a whole new approach to human interaction. It is a very big deal and "overnight success" is not in the cards.

To Do:
56
What is your level of preparation for your next meeting????? (If you "just don't have the damn time . . ." well, then, cancel the damn meeting. Rule #1: No mega-prep, no meeting.)

14.57

Leading-Getting Things Done Rule #1:

Spend 80 percent (!!!) of Your Time Recruiting and Nurturing Allies and Pursuing Small Wins

(Rule #2: See Rule #1)

Ally Recruitment and Development

The Iron Law

Losers . . . focus on (waste inordinate amounts of time on) enemies.
Winners . . . focus on allies, allies, and more allies.

Losers . . . focus on "removing roadblocks."
Winners . . . evade roadblocks and focus on "small wins" in out-of-the-way-places with new allies that are positive demos of the "new way."

Losers . . . make enemies.

Winners . . . make friends.

Losers . . . suck up to bosses.

Winners . . . suck down and make battalions of friend / allies where the work is actually done.

Losers . . . focus on negatives.

Winners . . . focus on positives.

Losers . . . stick out like a sore thumb.

Winners . . . work via allies (and give allies 99% of the credit for successes) and are largely invisible.

Losers . . . favor brute force and relish bloodshed.

Winners . . . quietly surround those who disagree with allies-of-every-flavor and small-wins-by-the-bushel.

In Conclusion:

Allies.
Allies. Allies.
More Allies.

This is personal: The program I developed at McKinsey & Company that led to *In Search of Excellence* flew directly in the face of McKinsey's core beliefs (strategy first, people stuff / culture a distant second). Hence my "enemies" were the proud organization's "power players," and I was definitely not a power player. My (eventually) winning strategy was, to the extent possible, forget the Bad Guys and Big Guys and recruit allies of every flavor in every nook and every cranny. In the spirit of the suggestion here, ally recruitment and development absorbed the lion's share of my time over the entire four years I was involved.

Relative to the project you are working on right now, what new supporters have you recruited . . . within the last week? (No glib answer, please.) "No time, I'm working on the project." Wrong! "Working on the project" = Recruiting new allies and keeping old allies up to date.

Allies are your life.

14.58

GTD / Getting Things Done

Power Tool #1: "Suck Down For Success"

"He [the principal protagonist] had become a legend with the people who manned the underbelly of the Agency [CIA]."

—George Crile, *Charlie Wilson's War*

Success and implementation excellence odds are directly proportional to the breadth and depth of your network two or three (or four) levels "down" in the organization. "Down there" is home to the (typically underappreciated) people who do the real nuts-and-bolts work of the organization. Invisible but all-important. And worthy of a great deal of your time and attention. And affection.

This point deserves to be separated from the rest of the GTD leadership ideas, and receive special notice:

"Sucking up" is for bureaucrats.
"Sucking down" is for winners / doers.

Bonus: Hanging out "down there" with those folks who do the real work is a helluva lot more enjoyable than time spent on suck-up rituals!

To Do:
58   Implementation of your (make or break) project will likely require the support of three or four departments. How strong is your network in the "boiler room" in each off those departments? No approximations, please.

14.59

Leading = Showtime

The *Real* Greatest Showman

"It's always showtime!"
—David D'Alessandro, *Career Warfare*

"It had been a scene that those in the room would long remember. Washington had performed his role to perfection. It was not enough that a leader look the part; by Washington's rules, he must know how to act it with self-command and precision. John Adams would later describe Washington approvingly as one of the 'great actors of the age'."
—David McCullough, *1776.*

When the situation in Boston was most dire for the ragtag Continental Army, Washington convinced the British, through a studied demeanor, a carefully constructed tableau (which made his HQ look grand and his Army appear hale and hearty and well equipped), signaling that the Americans were a formidable force to be reckoned with.

To Do:
59A

"Showmanship" might not seem very related to business, let alone winning a war (Washington). But it is. Maybe you are "only" a 1st-level boss. Well, the folks who work for you watch you like hawks. Is Nancye (or Jeffrey) in a good mood today or not? Etc. GTD / Getting Things Done is driven by the attitude you exhibit today, more than by the so-called "substance." Be aware of, in particular, your emotional footprint! FYI: "Showmanship" means being aware you are "on stage" and making an impression of one sort or another. It is not about raising your voice and wildly waving your arms. Arguably, "quiet showmanship" is more powerful than noisy showmanship. See below.

Leading = Showtime

Dispensing Enthusiasm (Or Not)

The Stunning Power of Body Language

"I am a dispenser of enthusiasm."

—Ben Zander, symphony conductor and management guru

The musical score is invariant; the quality of the performance is largely determined by the energy / enthusiasm / love transmitted by the conductor. So, too, in every organizational setting. And a repeat: Enthusiasm does *not* equate with noisy!

Leaders *are* showmen.
All leaders are showmen.
All leaders are showmen *all* the time.
No option.
Never off stage.
Be *prepared*.

"Research indicates the pitch, volume and pace of your voice affect what people think you said about five times as much as the actual words you used."

—Prof. Deborah Gruenfeld, "Behavior Lessons for Leadership and Teamwork," *Stanford Business*

5x!

To Do: 59B

Re-read the quote immediately above. Re-read it perhaps five times. S-l-o-w-l-y. Let it sink in. Body language beats substance 5:1. You are a leader. You must become aware of how you come across in terms of body language. You probably didn't study this in school unless you were a theater major. (Yes, I repeat, we need more theater majors in our companies.) So become a body-language student on your own. Become self-aware. Ask a close friend for feedback. Remember: 5:1. This is a . . . big deal!

To Do: 59C

The "watch your body language" dictum would seem to go by the wayside in WFH / Zoom world. Not so! Different, but just as important. The arms and legs may disappear, but facial expression is more important than ever. Work on it!

14.60

Loving Leading (Or Not)

He said I had left something out in my leadership spiel . . .
"Tom, it was a fine speech, but you left out the most important thing . . . Leaders enjoy leading!"

I'd given a speech in Dublin titled "The Leadership 50;" the content was 50 attributes of effective leadership. Afterwards, and over a Guinness of course, the head of a sizeable marketing-services firm made the above remark about what I had omitted.

As I reflected, I agreed he was on the money. Simply put: Some people "get off" on the people and politics puzzles, and thrive on the inherent messiness of human affairs that are at the heart of effective leadership.

Some don't.

Leading is its own thing.
And it may or may not, even after extensive study and coaching, be your thing.
Think long and hard about this.
This applies to a four-week assignment as project leader of a four-person team as much as it does to a "big" job.

I'm afraid that "leading, love it or leave it" is a pretty accurate summation.

To Do:
60   Think about it. Think about what leading really means, the things you-as-leader must worry about. Do you really like working with people; do you "get off" on human peculiarities; or do they more often than not annoy you? I am not urging a "yes" / "no" decision. I am asking for self-reflection. Remember what my Dublin pal said: loving to lead is an imperative, in fact, per his assessment, Imperative #1 for effective leadership. He has a point.

14.61

Leading

Unscheduled Time
(Lots Of)

The Fifty-Percent
Aspiration

A Must / No Option

"Avoid busy-ness, free up your time, stay focused on what really matters. Let me put it bluntly: every leader should routinely keep a substantial portion of his or her time—I would say as much as 50 percent—unscheduled . . .
Only when you have substantial 'slop' in your schedule—unscheduled time—will you have the space to reflect on what you are doing, learn from experience, and recover from your inevitable mistakes."

—Dov Frohman, Intel superstar, *Leadership the Hard Way: Why Leadership Can't Be Taught and How You Can Learn It.*

The main point, as I see it: Effective leadership is thoughtful leadership. And thoughtfulness, thinking in general, goes to hell amidst an overcrowded schedule. So do the little touches of care and concern that set the excellent leader and effective culture apart.

Related, from Frank Partnoy's *Wait: The Art and Science of Delay*:

"Thinking about the role of delay is a profound and fundamental part of being human. . . . The amount of time we take to reflect on decisions will define who we are.

Life might be a race against time, but it is enriched when we rise above our instincts and stop the clock to process and understand what we are doing and why."

Yes, an entire book on "waiting." Novel and, for my money, meriting the word "profound." Frohman plus Partnoy: pay attention.

To Do: 61   So, can you do it, get to fifty percent unscheduled? Probably not—but you *can* do your damnedest to raise your ten percent (or less, I'd bet) to, say, twenty percent. There are very few, if any, "To Dos" in this book that are more important than this one.

14.62

Leading / Reading (And Reading, Reading . . .)

"In my whole life, I have known no wise people (over a broad subject matter area) who didn't read all the time—none. ZERO. You'd be amazed at how much Warren [Buffett] reads—and how much I read."

—Charlie Munger (Vice Chairman, Berkshire Hathaway / Buffett's #2), *Poor Charlie's Almanack: The Wit and Wisdom of Charles T. Munger*

"If I had to pick the #1 failing of CEOs, it's that they don't read enough."

—Co-founder of one of the world's largest investment companies, in a conversation with me.

Number One failing . . . a surprise, "knock me over with a feather," comment!
Please do not idly flip past this.
Please consider carefully.
Repeat: #1-CEO-failing.

READ.
READ.
READ. . . .

To Do: 62   Reading rules:

Breadth! Breadth! Breadth! The main idea is to open your mind and broaden your scope of knowledge. Creativity is a by-product of breadth. 10× more than depth. Pulling ideas from arenas brand new to you and translating them into your sphere of interest is key. (This is not a mechanical act. I'm talking about subconscious novel connections that sneak in when you are, say, dealing with thorny issues.)

Read fiction. Fiction is all about people and relationships. This and that cause your mind to expand and productively wander in ways that are invaluable, but of which you are unaware.

Subliminal impact. Your mind is broadened. And somehow or other, the new things you've been examining in your reading sneak into your way of being and impact your practical, and long-term strategic, actions.

And in your areas of expertise, outread the buggers. You never know nearly as much as you think you know about much of what you do. (It is a matter of brute force for me. Stay near the head of my class, one book at a time.)

Winning Strategy 2021: Intense studenthood-in-perpetuity.

If you're the boss, occasionally ask Maria or Jackson, "What have you read that's interesting lately? Should I read it?"

If you're the boss, consider a book club, preferably on topic about which you and your teammates know very little—it's all about thinking and, I repeat, broadening horizons.

Aim for your team to be "Best-in-Industry" when it comes to reading and studying and learning.

14.63

Leader Skill #1 & Core Value #1

"Aggressive" Listening / "Fierce" Listening

"My education in leadership began in Washington when I was an assistant to Defense Secretary William Perry. He was universally loved and admired by heads of state . . . and our own and allied troops. A lot of that was because of the way he listened. Each person who talked to him had his complete, undivided attention. Everyone blossomed in his presence, because he was so respectful, and I realized I wanted to affect people the same way.

Perry became my role model, but that was not enough. Something bigger had to happen, and it did. It was painful for me to realize how often I just pretended to hear people. How many times had I barely glanced up from my work when a subordinate came into my office. . . .

I vowed to treat every encounter with every person on the Benfold [Abrashoff was Captain of the USS Benfold] as the most important thing at that moment . . . I decided that my job was to listen aggressively."

—Mike Abrashoff, *It's Your Ship: Management Techniques from the Best Damn Ship in the Navy*

Key word: *"Aggressively"*: Listening is *not* a passive activity!

"It's amazing how this seemingly small thing—simply paying fierce attention to another, really asking, really listening, even during a brief conversation—can evoke such a wholehearted response."

—Susan Scott, *Fierce Conversations: Achieving Success at Work and in Life, One Conversation at a Time*

Key word: *"Fierce."* Repeat: listening is *not* a passive activity!

"When I left the dining room after sitting next to Gladstone, I thought he was the cleverest man in England. But when I sat next to Disraeli, I left feeling that I was the cleverest woman!"

—Jennie Jerome, Winston Churchill's (American) mother, in *Disraeli*, by Christopher Hibbert

To Do: 63A   Think about the words "aggressive" and "fierce" as prefixes for "listening." "Intense concentration" (without let up) when you are listening to the other person is a start. But what would "aggressive" listening or "fierce" listening translate into? The next time you are with someone and they are speaking, let the words "aggressive" and "fierce" run through your mind.

Ear Power

"The best way to persuade people is with your ears, by listening to them."

—Former U.S. Secretary of State Dean Rusk

My opinion: This ought to be on a T-shirt, on a poster behind every boss' desk!

Branson: The Matchless Importance of Listening

Fully one third, the entirety of "Part One," over 100 pages, of Richard Branson's book, *The Virgin Way: How to Listen, Learn, Laugh, and Lead*, is devoted to listening per se.

Flavor of the book: *"The key to every one of these [eight] leadership attributes was the vital importance of a leader's ability to listen."*

I have never seen anything comparable to this.

Listening Excellence. *Not.*

Jerome Groopman, physician and Harvard Medical School professor, wrote the book *How Doctors Think*. He asserts that the key to collecting useful information and dealing effectively with the patient's health puzzle is to let the patient ramble through a description of her or his problem. Yet Groopman cites solid research that paints a rather sorry picture.

The average doctor interrupts the patient after . . . *18 seconds.*
S-E-C-O-N-D-S!

Over to you dear reader . . .

To Do:
63B
Are you (Boss / Leader), in your world, an . . . "18-second interrupter"? (Get serious and regular feedback on this. Your self-perception is likely [almost surely] waaaaay off.)

If you *are* an 18-second interrupter:

Get to work (and work / hard work it is).
Feedback is essential.
Start time: Now!

Listening is

An obsession with listening is:

. . . the ultimate mark of respect.
. . . the heart and soul of engagement and thoughtfulness.
. . . the basis for collaboration and partnership and community.
. . . a developable individual skill. (Though women are inherently far better at it than men.)
. . . the core of effective cross-functional communication (which is in turn arguably Attribute #1 of organization effectiveness).
. . . the key to making the sale.
. . . the key to keeping the customer's business.
. . . the linchpin of memorable service.
. . . the core of taking diverse opinions aboard.
. . . profitable. (The "R.O.I." from listening is arguably higher than from any other single activity!)
. . . the bedrock that underpins a genuine commitment to excellence.

Not a smidgeon of overstatement in this list.

242 | Leading with Compassion and Care

The Good Listener's Rules
(A Sampler)

A good listener exists totally for the given conversation. There is nothing else on earth of any importance to me for these (five, 10, 30) minutes.

To borrow from Susan Scott again: Listening success = Fierce attentiveness.

A good listener gives the other person time to . . . stumble toward clarity . . . without interruption. (A 10- or 20-second awkward pause, a 45-second pause, when someone is . . . thinking-before-talking . . . is not an invitation to interrupt. *Damn it.*)

A good listener *never* finishes the other person's sentence.

A good listener becomes *invisible*; makes the respondent the centerpiece.

A good listener does not *ever* take a call, even from their boss.

A good listener takes (*extensive*) notes.

A good listener *calls* (better than email . . . damn it) a couple of hours later to thank the other for their time.

A good listener calls the next day with a couple of follow-up queries.

A good listener does *not* pontificate!

Axiom: *If you ain't exhausted after a serious conversation, then you weren't really listening.*

Listening Excellence

Suggested Core Value #1: "We Are Effective Listeners." We Treat Listening EXCELLENCE as the Centerpiece of Our Commitment to Respect and Engagement and Community and Customer-connectedness and Growth.

The Last Word on Listening

"Never miss a good chance to shut up."
—Will Rogers

14.64

The Speed Trap /
S-L-O-W D-O-W-N

The word on the street:
"These are crazy times / There's a 'disruption'-a-day.
Pant. Pant. Pant.
Speed is the key to personal success.
Speed is the key to enterprise success.
Speed. Speed. More speed . . ."

So speed is the key to all good things circa the 2020s???

Hold on . . .

Below is a partial list of strategic activities—that underpin both personal and organizational success and excellence— which cannot be accomplished in a flash (or, for that matter, 100 flashes):

Building / maintaining relationships . . . takes (lots and lots . . . and lots!) of time.
Recruiting allies to your cause . . . takes (lots of) time.
Building / maintaining a high-performance culture . . . takes (lots and lots) of time.
Reading / studying . . . takes (lots of) time.
Fierce / aggressive listening . . . takes (lots of) time.

MBWA / Managing By Wandering Around . . . takes (lots of) time.

Slack in your schedule . . . takes (lots of) time.

Hiring / evaluating / promoting . . . takes (lots of) time.

Thoughtfulness / collective instinctive small gestures (Small > Big) . . . takes (lots of) time.

Extreme Humanism / emotional connective design . . . takes (lots and lots of) time.

Your next excellent email . . . *should* take (lots of) time.

The "last one percent" of any task or project . . . takes (lots of) time.

E-x-c-e-l-l-e-n-c-e . . . takes (lots and lots . . . and lots of!) time.

To Do: 64 "Bottom line": Rome was not built in a day, nor is Enterprise Excellence. SLOW DOWN.

14.65

Frequently (And Stupidly) Neglected . . .

"Quiet Power"

Hire Quiet

Promote Quiet

Noisy People Are Not the Most Creative People

Noisy People Are Not the Best Salespeople

Noisy People Are Not the Best Leaders

From *Quiet: The Power of Introverts in a World That Can't Stop Talking*, by Susan Cain:

1. THE (VERY) (QUESTIONABLE) EXTROVERT IDEAL: *"The Extrovert Ideal has been documented in many studies. . . . Talkative people, for example, are rated as smarter, better looking, more interesting, and more desirable as friends. Velocity of speech counts as well as volume: we rank fast talkers as more competent and likeable than slow ones. . . . But we make a grave mistake to embrace the Extrovert Ideal so unthinkingly."*

2. CONVERSATIONAL PAIRINGS EXPERIMENT: *"The introverts and extroverts participated about equally, giving the lie to the idea that introverts talk less. But the introvert pairs tended to focus on one or two serious subjects of conversation, while the extrovert pairs were lighter-hearted and surfaced wider-ranging topics."*

3. LIMITS TO ASSERTIVENESS: "Also remember the dangers of the new groupthink. If it's creativity you're after, ask your employees to solve problems alone before sharing their ideas . . . Don't mistake assertiveness or elegance for good ideas. If you have a proactive workforce (and I hope you do), remember that they may perform better under an introverted leader than under an extroverted or charismatic one."

4. QUIET POWER: "The next time you see a person with a composed face and a soft voice, remember that inside her mind she might be solving an equation, composing a sonnet, designing a hat. She might, that is, be deploying the power of quiet."

My take on Ms. Cain's powerful book: "We" [leaders] have given short shrift to almost half the population—the half that is often more thoughtful than their noisy peers and, the research shows, make better leaders as well. Unleashing "quiet power" is a (GSO) Grand *Strategic* Opportunity.

Regarding noisy / quiet, I am reminded of Peter Drucker's deep skepticism concerning "charisma." He flatly did not think charisma contributed to effective organizational leadership— and pointed out that the political leaders who had caused the most harm were, however, almost unfailingly "charismatic."

To Do:
65

1. Read the book *Quiet* slowly—and reflect. Please.

2. Starting today (!), bend over backwards to inject a conscious "quiet bias" into all you do, particularly hiring and promotion decisions.

3. Going forward in accordance with Ms. Cain's argument would have us go against our basic instincts, which in turn means you'll have to work like hell to overcome your biases. The great news, of course: *The payoff is enormous.*

(FYI: *Quiet* is my pick as best business book of the century to date. For heaven's sake, we are talking about no less than our implicit bias against almost half of the population. And the fact that the underattended half, once given the chance, outperform their noisy peers!)

14.66

Positive Beats Negative 30:1!

Acknowledgment = The Most Powerful Leadership "Tool"

"Positive attention is thirty times more powerful than negative attention in creating high performance on a team. So while we may occasionally have to help people get better at something, if paying attention to what people can't do is our default setting as team leaders, and if all our efforts are directed at giving and receiving negative feedback more often and more efficiently, then we're leaving enormous potential on the table. People don't need feedback. They need attention, and, moreover, attention to what they do the best. And they become more engaged and therefore more productive when we give it to them."

—Marcus Buckingham and Ashley Goodall, *Nine Lies About Work: A Freethinking Leader's Guide to the Real World*, from Chapter Five, "Lie #5: People Need Feedback"

Re-read this. Then re-re-read. **30×!** *Why do so relatively few get the staggering power of positive attention / feedback?*

I am eternally puzzled. And I'd add that the *negative* feedback that 9.86 out of 10 bosses give is done in a ham-handed, destructive way. And I'd also further note that the authors are hard-nosed, meticulous, lifelong quant researchers; this defines trustworthy—no approximations here.

"The deepest principle in human nature is the craving to be appreciated."
—William James, philosopher

V-e-r-y strong language! V-e-r-y merited*!*

"The two most powerful things in existence: a kind word and a thoughtful gesture."
—Ken Langone, co-founder, Home Depot

"People who don't feel significant rarely make significant contributions."
—Mark Sanborn, author and sales guru

Repetitive quotes. For a reason. Frustration. Frustration at my continuing inability to make this (one more time: "not rocket science") message stick.

To Do: **66A**	POSITIVE. POSITIVE. POSITIVE. (RIGHT NOW.) POSITIVE. POSITIVE. POSITIVE. POSITIVE. (DAMN IT.)

"Leadership is about how you make people feel—about you, about the project or work you're doing together, and especially about themselves."

—Betsy Myers, *Take the Lead: Motivate, Inspire, and Bring Out the Best in Yourself and Everyone Around You*

WDYT / WHAT DO *YOU* THINK?

"What do you think?"

—Dave Wheeler, organizational effectiveness expert, calls WDYT the "four most important words in the leaders vocabulary"

Not only do I wholeheartedly agree with Mr. Wheeler, but I suggest that you keep a literal count of your *"Daily WDYTs."* At the least, it will remind you of the importance of those Big-Four-Words.

To Do:
66B   Count your "WDYTs." Start today . . .

"I call 60 CEOs [in the first week of the year] to wish them happy New Year."

—Hank Paulson, former CEO, Goldman Sachs / former U.S. Secretary of the Treasury

Since 1973, and without fail, I have practiced a version of this. I religiously make between 25 and 50 "I deeply appreciate your support this past year" calls at Christmas / New Year's. The positive feedback is nothing short of astounding, which of course, confirms the rarity and power of such a practice. (And it is an annual highlight. I enjoy it immensely!)

To Do:
66C   Try some version of this. It works! (And it's also a delight to do—for both parties.)

My "Bottom line" on "all this":

"Acknowledgement" may be the most powerful word in the English language – and it's counterpart in any language.

Frustration alert. I really *really* am at my wits end. Why oh why oh why is inducing people to "go positive" such a hard sell?

Does it make you "soft" to say something nice? Do people really need "straight talk" (tough-minded negative feedback) in order to perform better?

I-J-U-S-T-D-O-N'-T-G-E-T-I-T.

14.67

Thank You:
The "30K Rule"

"Believe it or not, I have sent roughly 30,000 handwritten notes to employees . . . over the last decade, from maintenance people to senior executives."

— Douglas Conant, "Secrets of Positive Feedback" *Harvard Business Review*

That amounts to approximately . . . 11 handwritten thank you notes every weekday for . . . 10 years. Nothing short of amazing!

"Thank you" power? INFINITE.
Yes . . . I-N-F-I-N-I-T-E.

Thank You: "Little" > "Big"
One More Time—A Persistent Theme

It's not the "Thank you" for making the million-dollar sale that matters. Praise for that's going to happen regardless! It's, to use Ken Blanchard's term, "catching someone doing something [some little thing] right."

To the recipient, the spontaneous kudo for the "little ones" has higher and more lasting impact than the biggies. It means that you, leader, noticed the wee act. You have made the recipient— recall the earlier quote—feel significant.

Significant = Mighty Motivator.

To Do: 67 What is your TTYC / Tiny "Thank You" Count . . . in the last four hours? (This is a damned serious question.)

14.68

Apology Works

The Magical "Three-Minute Call"

Apology Pays

"I regard apologizing as the most magical, healing, restorative gesture human beings can make. It is the centerpiece of my work with executives who want to get better."

—Marshall Goldsmith, *What Got You Here Won't Get You There: How Successful People Become Even More Successful*

Re-read. Focus and reflect on apology as "centerpiece." A powerful and unequivocal word! This genuinely surprised me, apology as "centerpiece" of executive coaching, and the source, Marshall Goldsmith, is unimpeachable.

The Apology Iron Law
The "Three-Minute Rule"

The Apology Iron Law: There once was a point in time when you could have headed off a first-order fiasco (e.g., billion $$ sale loss) with an apologetic three-minute drop by or three-minute phone call within a few minutes or hours of the infraction in question arising.

Do it now.
Nooow.
Noooooow.

Apology Pays / $$$
From John Kador, *Effective Apology*

Yes. An entire book on apology per se!!! Message: One can become a full-fledged student of critical "soft" topics such as . . . Apology.

From the book:

1. *"Consider the example of Toro, the lawn mower and snowblower manufacturer. Toro switched to a more conciliatory approach that always begins with an apology from the company, regardless of who's at fault. The company hasn't been to trial since 1994 [written in 2009] and has cut the average cost [of settling a claim] from $115,000 in 1991 to $35,000 in 2008."*

2. *"Today, more and more, doctors and hospitals realize that a coordinated program of disclosure and apology dramatically reduces malpractice claims. In the year 2000, the mean national VA [hospital] malpractice*

judgment was $413,000. Lexington's [VA hospital using the disclosure and apology method] mean payment was $36,000."

Read Mr. Kador's superb book. Become—YES—a formal student of apology / apology power. Talk about this with colleagues as an Enterprise Cultural Trait. Make timely apology an accepted part of our Organizational Character.

14.69

Self-Knowledge: Leader Differentiator #1

The Quality of Your Self-Perception Stinks

"Being aware of yourself and how you affect everyone around you is what distinguishes a superior leader."

—Cindy Miller, with Edie Seashore, in "Masters of the Breakthrough Moment," *Strategy + Business*

Edie Seashore knew few if any peers in the world of Organizational Development. The Miller-Seashore assertion here is a strong one: *When it comes to effective leadership, they assert, self-knowledge is the #1 distinguishing trait.* They are hardly alone in this belief. Arguably, the majority of the top leadership experts would use language as strong, or almost as strong; that is, self- knowledge as Leader Strength #1. Ponder that. *Please.*

"To develop others, start with yourself."
—Marshall Goldsmith

"Work on me first."
—Kerry Patterson, Joseph Grenny, Ron McMillan and Al Switzler, *Crucial Conversations: Tools for Talking When Stakes are High*

"Leadership is self-knowledge. Successful leaders are those who are conscious about their behavior and the impact it has on the people around them. They are willing to examine what behaviors of their own may be getting in the way. The toughest person you will ever lead is yourself. We can't effectively lead others unless we can lead ourselves."
—Betsy Myers, *Take the Lead: Motivate, Inspire, and Bring Out the Best in Yourself and Everyone Aroun*

"How can a high-level leader like _____ [name not provided by the author] be so out of touch with the truth about himself? It's more common than you would imagine. In fact, the higher up the ladder a leader climbs, the less accurate his self-assessment is likely to be. The problem is an acute lack of feedback [especially on people issues]."
—Daniel Goleman et al., *Primal Leadership: Unleashing the Power of Emotional Intelligence*

This Daniel Goleman quote is consistent with a substantial body of research on leaders' misperceptions. In one quantitative study, the researcher meticulously counted the number of times a leader interrupted others in the course of a typical meeting, and the number of times the leader himself was interrupted. You can imagine the results: The leader felt he had rarely interrupted, but that he had been frequently interrupted. The data unequivocally say the reverse to a degree that would be laughable were the topic not so serious.

To Do: 69 Your self-perception is almost certainly wrong. (Wrong by 180 degrees in the case of a good friend—brilliant beyond measure intellectually and analytically, a total dunce when it came to understanding what others thought of him.) Get help from a trusted colleague or, if you can afford it, an executive coach. But by hook or by crook get a sound reading. Then act accordingly, with the help of that coach if possible. This is clearly a start-today-top-of-the-agenda item.

Leading / The Masters on Self-Management

"There are three things that are extremely hard: steel, a diamond, and to know one's self."
—Ben Franklin

"The biggest problem I shall ever face: the management of Dale Carnegie."
—Dale Carnegie

14.70

Leading / 14 = 14

Fourteen People = Fourteen Radically Different Communication Strategies

"The great enemy of communication is the illusion of it."
—William H. Whyte, "Is Anybody Listening?" *Fortune*

You have a team of fourteen people. How do you
"communicate" with them?
Forget "them."
Think: "Asma," "Ivan," "Jack" . . .

Fourteen people / team members means fourteen *very* distinct
communication / motivation / leadership strategies.

No two people are alike.
No two people are even close to being alike.
No one person is the same on Thursday as they
were on Monday.

Fourteen people.
Fourteen distinct leadership strategies.
PERIOD.
(And never forget it!)

To Do:
70 Do you buy this? (OMG, I hope so? It is a v-e-r-y b-i-g d-e-a-l.) So . . . do you have a significantly tailored communication strategy for each of the people who report to you on your team? (Note: Suppose you are a project manager of a team that will only exist for 10 weeks. Well, the "individually tailored communication strategy" is 10× more important than it would be if this were a permanent group. That is, with a 10-week duration, there is no room for error.

14.71

A Culture of Kindness

"Three things in human life are important. The first is to be kind. The second is to be kind. And the third is to be kind."
—Henry James

"Kindness Is Free"

"[There is a] misconception that supportive interactions require more staff or more time and are therefore more costly. Although labor costs are a substantial part of any hospital budget, more personalized interactions themselves add nothing to the budget. Listening to patients or answering their questions costs nothing. It can be argued that negative interactions—alienating patients, not advocating for their needs, limiting their sense of control —can be very costly. . . . Angry, frustrated or frightened patients may be combative, withdrawn and less cooperative, requiring far more time than it would have taken to interact with them initially in a positive way."

— JoAnne L. Earp, Elizabeth A. French, Melissa B. Gilkey, *Patient Advocacy for Health Care Quality: Strategies for Achieving Patient-Centered Care*

Kindness: The 40 Second Rule (or Is it 38 Seconds?)

From *Compassionomics: The Revolutionary Scientific Evidence That Caring Makes a Difference*, by Stephen Treciak, M.D. and Anthony Mazzarelli, M.D.:

In randomized controlled trials at Johns Hopkins with cancer patients, researchers found that all that was needed to make a meaningful difference in lessening patient anxiety and fear was forty seconds of compassion. Further, in two studies from the Netherlands Institute for Health Services Research in studying compassion and lack of compassion delivered with a cancer diagnosis, researchers found that it took only thirty-eight seconds to deliver the news compassionately making a "meaningful and measurable" difference in patients anxiety levels and ability to take in more information, not to mention treatment adherence covered also in their astounding book. And while doctors often say they don't have time for compassion, these and other studies consistently suggest something very very different.

To Do:
71A

How about you? Do you have 40 seconds? Or even 38 seconds to spare? That is, do you have time for kindness? Kindness in extreme situations in healthcare. Kindness in the average day at work. The results can be nothing short of stupendous.

K = R = P

Kindness = Repeat Business = Profit

There is a (BIG) problem with what has come before in this leadership section. Few of these ideas—apology, "thank you," kindness—work unless the leader is empathetic and thoughtful and deliberate; i.e., really gives a damn about people. (Back, in part, to my book opener, To Do #2 (on page 34), declaring that EQ was hiring requirement #1.) These "tactics" are, it is fair to say, wholly dependent upon the underlying character of the leader.

To Do:
71B

I'm not sure how to do a "TTD" for "kindness." "Be kind" is silly. So, let's take another tack: This is really about who you are as a person, and what kind of organization (or project team) you want to build, and what legacy you want to leave behind. Kindness does build repeat business and pay (K = R = P), but kindness in customer interactions is a direct byproduct of the way we treat one another hour-by-hour and day-by-day. So, my "TTD" is to ask you, please, to reflect on what kind of person you are and what kind of footprint you want to leave behind.

Read! Study! Civility! Kindness!

Kindness in Leadership, by Gay Haskins, Mike Thomas, and Lalit Johri

The Manager's Book of Decencies: How Small Gestures Build Great Companies, by Steve Harrison, Adecco

Mastering Civility: A Manifesto for the Workplace, by Christine Porath

The Power of Nice: How to Conquer the Business World with Kindness, by Linda Kaplan Thaler and Robin Koval

Survival of the Friendliest: Understanding Our Origins and Rediscovering Our Humanity, by Brian Hare and Vanessa Woods

14.72

Grace

For my 60th birthday, I wrote a book titled in full: *SIXTY*. Translation: Sixty things I really cared about. My closer, #60, was by definition a Big Deal. And it was but a single word: *Grace*.

My commentary started with a quote from renowned designer Celeste Cooper:

"My favorite word is grace—whether it's 'amazing grace,' 'saving grace,' 'grace under fire,' 'Grace Kelly.' How we live contributes to beauty—whether it's how we treat other people or how we treat the environment."

My synonym finder, *Rodale's*, offers these analogies to grace: *elegance . . . charm . . . loveliness . . . kindness . . . benevolence . . . benefaction . . . compassion . . . beauty.*

Grace in all we do. And the more rushed and harried and potentially insensitive we are, the more important grace is.

To Do:
72
Elegance . . .
Charm . . .
Loveliness . . .
Benevolence . . .
Benefaction . . .

Compassion . . .

Beauty.

Perhaps put this list on a card and carry it in your wallet. Pull it out a couple of times a day, especially when the stress seems to be winning. Read and breathe.

Grace is good for you. Grace is good for your teammates. "Grace in all we do" is especially pertinent, and powerful, in the face of the uncertainty and, indeed, chaos of Covid-19. Grace is enriching for your customers and your community—and, in the end, to make this "business-y," your bottom line.

14.73

Leader as "Chief Culture Officer"

Culture "*Is* the Game"

"If I could have chosen not to tackle the IBM culture head-on, I probably wouldn't have. . . . My bias coming

*in was toward strategy, analysis and measurement. . . .
In comparison, changing the attitude and behaviors of
hundreds of thousands of people is very, very hard to
accomplish. . . . Yet I came to see, in my time at IBM, that
culture isn't just one aspect of the game—it is the game."*

—Lou Gerstner, IBM turnaround superstar, *Who Says Elephants Can't Dance? Inside IBM's Historic Turnaround*

Gerstner was my nemesis when I was doing the *In Search of Excellence* research at McKinsey. He was perhaps the premier champion of "strategy first." Hence, you can imagine my smile of self-satisfaction when the quote above appeared in *Who Says Elephants Can't Dance: Leading a Great Enterprise Through Dramatic Change.*

"Culture eats strategy for breakfast."

—Ed Schein

**To Do:
73A**
"It *is* the game." FYI: "Culture" - good, bad, indifferent - applies to a temporary work team. Leading . . . anything? Make culture your business. Period.

The Culture Mandates

Culture comes first.

Culture is exceedingly difficult to change.

Culture change cannot be / must not be evaded or avoided.

Culture maintenance is about as difficult as culture change.

Culture change / maintenance must become a conscious / permanent / personal agenda item.

Culture change / maintenance is manifest in "the little things" far more than the big things.

Repeat.
Culture change / maintenance:
One day
One hour
One minute at a time.
Forever. And ever.

Leading / Culture Maintenance Small > Big (Again)

"Mary Ann Morris, who manages general services and Mayo Clinic volunteer programs at Mayo Rochester, likes to tell a story about her early days at the Clinic. She was working in a laboratory—a job that required her to wear a white uniform and white shoes. And after a frantic morning getting her two small children to school, she arrived at work to find her supervisor staring at her shoes. The supervisor had noticed that the laces were dirty where they threaded through the eyelets of the shoes and asked Morris to clean them. Offended, Morris said that she worked in a laboratory, not with patients, so why should it matter? Her supervisor replied that Morris had contact with patients in ways she didn't recognize— going out on the street wearing her Mayo name tag, for instance, or passing patients and their families as she walked through the halls—and that she couldn't represent Mayo Clinic with dirty shoelaces. 'Though I was initially offended, I realized over time [that] everything I do, down to my shoelaces, represents my commitment to

our patients and visitors. . . . I still use the dirty shoelace
story to set the standard for the service level I aspire to
for myself and my co-workers."'

—Leonard Berry & Kent Seltman, "Orchestrating the Clues of Quality," title, Chapter 7, from *Management Lessons from Mayo Clinic*

To Do:
73B

"Culture fanatics" (I hope you are one of them) focus on the "small stuff." How has that been manifest in your activities? T-O-D-A-Y?? (Specifics, please.)

Culture / Community Mindedness

Remember:

"Business exists to enhance human wellbeing."

—Mihaly Csikszentmihalyi, *Good Business: Leadership, Flow, and the Making of Meaning*

Business is imbedded in the community. Being a good neighbor is a profitable way to run a business.

And it is the right thing to do.

The right thing to do in terms of Extreme Employee Engagement (our people and their families as part of the community) and Community Citizen Support in general (all members of the community are de facto part of our business).

To Do:
73C

Put community-mindedness on your agenda. Explicitly. Regardless of what you do. Remember the earlier assertion: Business is not "part of" the community. Business is the community. (Community-consciousness should always be front and center.)

14.74

Leading with Excellence

Twenty-One Proven Tactics

1. "Give-a-Shit-ism" / You must care!

2. MBWA / Managing by Wandering Around. (Daily!)

3. MBZA / Managing By Zooming Around (Daily!)

4. Meetings. Meeting Prep. Meeting EXCELLENCE.

5. Ignore "Enemies." Ally-Friend Recruitment and Development. Eighty percent of Your Time.

6. Suck "DOWN" for Success. Tap Power in the Boiler Room.

7. It's Always Showtime! Dispense Enthusiasm!

8. Loving Leading (or Not).

9. Fifty percent Unscheduled Time.

10. Read. Read. Read. Read.

11. Aggressive-Fierce LISTENING / Listening EXCELLENCE = Core Value #1.

12. The Speed Trap. *Slow Down.* All the Important Stuff (Relationships, Excellence, etc.) Take (Lots of) Time.

13. "Quiet Power." Seek and Promote the Quiet Ones / Introverts = Better Leaders.

14. Positive Beats Negative 30:1.

15. "Thank You." *The* Most Important Habit. Small > Big.

16. Apology (Quick / Overwhelming) Works. Apology Pays.

17. Self-Knowledge = Leader Strength #1 (FYI: Your Self-Perception Stinks!)

18. 14 = 14 / 14 People = 14 (Dramatically Different) Communication Strategies.

19. A "Culture of Kindness." K = R = P / Kindness = Repeat Business = Profit. Bedrock for Most of the Above Tactics.

20. Grace.

21. Leader as "Chief Culture Officer." Culture Maintenance = Fulltime Job.

15

Executive Summary

Excellence Now:
The Forty-Three
Number Ones

15.75

Excellence Now:
The Forty-Three
Number Ones

Forty-three years chasing Excellence. Forty-three key ideas. Forty-three challenges. Forty-three opportunities. No linear order—each of these is a true "Number One."

Capital Investment #1: Training! Training! Training! That's right: capital investment, not "business expense." If you think that sounds extreme, ask an admiral, general, fire chief, police chief, football coach, archery coach, theater director, nuclear power plant operations boss, or head of an ER or ICU (or a public speaker—me).

Axiom #1: Hard (plans, org charts, numbers) is soft (abstract, easy to manipulate). Soft (people, relationships, culture) is hard (bedrock, stay-the-course). *Hard is soft. Soft is hard.* My raison d'être for the last forty-three years in six words.

Commandment #1: Excellence is *not* an "aspiration." Excellence is *not* a "hill to climb." Excellence *is* the next five minutes. Your next email. Your next meeting—real or virtual. Your next fleeting exchange with a customer. Or it is nothing at all.

Obsession #1: "Strategy is a commodity. Execution is an art." / Peter Drucker. "Amateurs talk about strategy. Professionals talk about logistics." / General R.H. Barrow. "Don't forget to tuck the shower curtain into the bathtub." / Conrad Hilton on "success secret number one." Execution, often the taken for granted grunt work, is the "last ninety-five percent."

Job #1: Establish and maintain a people *really* first culture. "Business has to give people enriching, rewarding lives . . . or it's simply not worth doing." / Richard Branson. "Your customers will never be any happier than your employees." / John DiJulius, customer service guru. Anatomy of enterprise: *People (leaders) serving people (front-line staff) serving people (customers and communities)*. Gold standard: "E-cubed" = Extreme Employee Engagement.

"Ism" #1: "Give-a-shit-ism." All the words and suggestions and commandments about "people first" are bad jokes unless the leader "gives a shit" about people to begin with. As I subsequently point out, deeply and demonstratively caring about people per se is clearly Consideration #1 in promotion decisions into any leadership position, including small-team project management. And hard evidence on the leader-candidate's GQ / Give-a-shit Quotient must be assiduously collected.

Vocabulary Erasure Task #1: Permanently remove "HR" / "Human Resources" from your vocabulary. Workers are, one hopes, turned-on, dedicated-to-growth contributors with names like Malia or Max, not nameless "human resources" (or "assets") from whom to extract maximum productivity until they are replaced by robots or AI and taken to the human junkyard.

Calling #1: Leading = Maximizing human potential. There is no higher calling. Operating definition: A great manager is literally *desperate* to have each of her team members succeed and grow and flourish. "The role of the director is to create a space where actors and actresses can become more than they have ever been before, more than they have ever dreamed of being." / Oscar-winning director Robert Altman.

Moral obligation #1: Leave no stone unturned in preparing workers, including part-timers, as best you can for a mad, mad world. "Business exists to enhance human wellbeing." / Mihaly Csikszentmihalyi

Leadership Team Must #1: "Research by McKinsey & Company suggests that to succeed, start by promoting women." / Nicholas Kristof. "Women are rated higher in fully twelve of sixteen competencies that go into outstanding leadership." / *Harvard Business Review.* The literature is clear: women are better leaders. Case closed. No screwing around. Put many, many more women in charge and in particular in senior-manager-executive-board positions. Now. Near-term goal: your board is over 50 percent female in two years.

Enterprise Strength #1: "In great armies, the job of generals is to back up their sergeants." / Army Colonel Tom Wilhelm. Front-line managers overwhelmingly drive *all* key productivity, product and service quality, employee retention, employee engagement, employee development, and innovation variables. Hence: Strength #1. Act accordingly!

Hiring Requirement #1: "We only hire nice people." / biotech CEO Peter Miller. "We look for people that are warm and caring and actually altruistic. We look for people who have a fun-loving attitude." / Colleen Barrett, Southwest Airlines. Hire first and foremost for EQ, empathy, and "soft skills" in 100 percent of jobs. Internal Google employee- and team-effectiveness research suggests that soft-skills-come-first holds in their rarefied tech air as much as it does for hoteliers or restauranteurs!

Promotion Requirement #1: Leader selection, especially frontline leader jobs, is the most important class of *strategic* decisions management makes. Drucker said promotions are "life-or-death decisions." Once again 10x: EQ / "soft skills" rule!

Core Value #1: Listening excellence. Listening = Engagement. Listening = Respect. Listening = Learning. Listening = Closing the sale. This isn't passive listening; it's "aggressive listening" per Navy Captain Mike Abrashoff. "The best way to persuade people is with your ears." / former Secretary of State Dean Rusk. "Never miss a good chance to shut up." / Will Rogers.

State of Mind #1: Excellent organizations are first and foremost vibrant communities. And communities that are embedded in communities. Requisite action: Extreme Community Engagement. Please reflect deeply on the idea of "community."

Racial Equality Obligation Opportunity #1: Acknowledge and erase inequality, guaranteed to be more present than you think within your organization's walls. Put a bold next-steps plan in place ASAP. Everyone must be involved. For one thing: executive team composition, in reasonably short order, must mirror the population. "I appreciate your Black Lives Matter post. Now follow that up with a picture of your senior management team and your board." / Brickson Diamond, CEO, diversity consulting firm Big Answers.

Value-added Strategy #1, Differentiator #1, Humanism hallmark #1, AI tamer #1: Design Excellence equals Extreme Humanism; products and services, internal as well as external, with heart and soul and spirit, which make the world a little bit better and which make us proud. "Design is the fundamental soul of a manmade creation." / Steve Jobs. "In some way, by caring, we are actually serving humanity. People might think it's a stupid belief, but it's a goal—it's a contribution that we hope we can make, in some small way, to culture." / Jony Ive, chief designer, Apple. Action: nothing less than making design-mindedness a way of life and a part of every decision in every nook and cranny will suffice. "Only one company can be the cheapest. All others must use design." / Rodney Fitch, CEO, UK design company.

Value-added Tiny Tactic #1: Small > Big. TGRs / Things Gone Right. "Small touches" are the ones that stick in the mind and stay there. "Courtesies of a small and trivial character are the ones which strike deepest in the grateful and appreciating heart." / Henry Clay. "We don't remember the days, we remember the moments." / Cesare Pavese. TGR-ing as a passion for one and all.

Value-added Success Credo #1: "The Three Rules: 1. Better before cheaper. 2. Revenue before cost. 3. There are no other rules." These rules were the conclusions from a Deloitte study of twenty-seven top performing companies extracted from a sample of 25,000 firms.

Global Imperative #1: Commit to Extreme Sustainability. No excuses, not a minute to lose. Sustainability should be part of virtually every decision, especially design decisions. "Sustainability is the right thing to do, the smart thing to do, the profitable thing to do." / Hunter Lovins. "Buy less, choose well, make it last. Quality rather than quantity. That is true sustainability." / Vivienne Westwood.

Social Media Engagement Must #1: "I would rather engage in a Twitter conversation with a single customer than see our company attempt to attract the attention of millions in a coveted Super Bowl commercial." / CEO of Tangerine, star Canadian financial services firm. "It takes 20 years to build a reputation and five minutes to ruin it." / John DiJulius. To a large extent, your social media strategy is you. Act big, act fast, act accordingly.

Extremism Necessity #1: My passions and proprietary domain names:

ExtremeHumanism.com.
ExtremeSustainability.com.
ExtremeCommunityEngagement.com.
ExtremeEmployeeEngagement.com.
ExtremeDesignMindfulness.com.
RadicalPersonalDevelopment.com.
HumanismOffensive.com.
FierceListening.com.
AggressiveListening.com.

Business Development Opportunity #1: "Forget China, India, and the internet: Economic growth is driven by women." / *Economist*. "Women are *the* majority market." / Fara Warner. Women buy everything—*everything*. Wise up. You may believe it, but do you act accordingly? Strategic realignment required!

Missed Market Opportunity #1: "People turning 50 today have half their adult lives ahead of them." / AARP's Bill Novelli. Oldies have *all* the money and plenty of time left to spend it. Wise up. Act accordingly. Current state of addressing the EOMO / Enormous Oldies Market Opportunity: marketers and product developers are clueless-dismissive-young-and-AWOL = Stupid. Strategic realignment required!

Economic Cornerstone #1: SMEs / Small- and Medium-size Enterprises employ almost all of us, create almost all new jobs, are the source of almost all innovation, and are the primary home of excellence. Celebrate them. Nurture them. Learn from them.

Innovation Lodestone #1: WTTMSW / Whoever Tries The Most Stuff Wins. Expanded version: WTTMS (ASTMSUTF) W / Whoever Tries The Most Stuff (And Screws The Most Stuff Up The Fastest) Wins. WTTMSW requisite culture: "Fail faster. Succeed sooner." / David Kelley. "Fail. Forward. Fast." / high-tech CEO. "Fail again. Fail better." / Samuel Beckett. Prerequisite: An inclusive "culture of serious play," as MIT innovation guru Michael Schrage puts it. 100 percent participating, 100 percent innovators!

Innovation Weirdification Requirement #1: Whoever has the most and weirdest weirdos, in every nook and cranny in the enterprise, wins the Great Game of Innovation. "Same-same" equals death to innovation. According to well-vetted innovation research by Scott Page, "Diversity trumps ability." Start by weirdifying the board of directors. Now.

Innovation Leadership Mindset #1: "We are crazy. We should only do something when people say it is 'crazy.' If people say something is 'good,' it means someone else is already doing it." / Canon CEO. "I'm uncomfortable when I'm comfortable." / advertising legend Jay Chiat. "Learn not to be careful." / photographer Diane Arbus. "If things seem under control, you're just not going fast enough." / race car driver Mario Andretti.

AI as Friend, Not Foe Mindset #1: Don't think for a moment that the emphasis on people denies the tech tsunami that is engulfing us. There are two ways to look at AI: Autonomous (no humans) Intelligence versus Intelligence Augmented (AI vs. IA). AuraPortal, the remote working and business productivity software company, describes this tug-of-war: "While artificial intelligence is the creation of machines to work and react like humans, augmented intelligence is using those same machines with a different approach—to enhance the human worker." Walk, don't run: consider the AI-IA options and configurations and systemic impact with extreme care.

Daily Strategic Activity #1: MBWA / Managing By Wandering Around. MBWA is the centerpiece of a true "people first" culture, and was, effectively, the centerpiece of *In Search of Excellence*. MBWA should be joy, not toil. If you don't love MBWA, find another job. Addenda 2021: MBZA / Managing By Zooming Around, can, with determination and practice, bring the same engaging spirit and spontaneity and intimacy to Zoomworld that MBWA at its best brings when you're F2F / Face to Face!

Time Management Must #1: We're living in the "age of disruption." Pant. Pant. Pant. Whoa: *Slow down*. All great things—relationships, excellence, world-altering design, quality—take time, and lots of it. And per Intel superstar Dov Frohman, leaders should religiously keep 50 percent (!) of their time unscheduled.

Time Investment #1: The best relationships, breadth and depth, drive all success. "Personal relationships are the fertile soil from which *all* advancement, *all* success, *all* achievement in real life grow." / investment superstar Ben Stein. Relationship excellence takes time, time, time. And more time. The hallmark of getting things done is relationships where the work is actually done. Message: Suck *down* (not up) for success.

Radical Change Key #1: *Make friends. Ignore enemies.* Want radical change? Avoid those who disagree. Commit 80 percent (yes, 80 percent!) of your time to enlisting and developing and nurturing allies. Fighting is a waste of time and mental energy, and in more than nine out of 10 cases, it backfires. Develop a Committed and Spirited and Tireless and Action-Obsessed Band of Sisters and Brothers . . . and surround the dissidents!

Performance Timeframe #1: Long > Short. Accumulated world-class research affirms that firms managed for the long-term *wildly* (correct word) outperform those focused on the next quarterly earnings numbers. The 50-year-old "only the next 90 days matter," Maximize Shareholder Value religion has been the most destructive—and wrongheaded—force in world business and, for that matter, society as a whole. "The very people we rely on to make investments in the productive capabilities that will increase our shared prosperity are instead devoting most of their companies' profit to uses that will increase their own prosperity." / economist William Lazonick.

Hallmark #1: Culture conquers all: "Culture eats strategy for breakfast." / MIT's Ed Schein. "Culture isn't just one aspect of the game—it *is* the game." / IBM chief Lou Gerstner. Culture development and maintenance comes first. Culture maintenance must be a one-minute-at-a-time obsession. Forever. And ever.

Power Word #1: *Acknowledgment* is the most powerful word in the language, and the most powerful tool in the leader's kit. "The two most powerful things in existence: a kind word and a thoughtful gesture." / Home Depot co-founder Ken Langone. Most powerful *two* words: "Thank you." Consistent small thank-yous beat big thank-yous. Thank-you mania moves mountains!

"Golden Thirty" Ratio #1: "Positive attention is thirty times more powerful than negative attention in creating high performance on a team." / Marcus Buckingham and Ashley Goodall. Conclusion: Positive (appreciation, helpfulness, supportiveness) beats negative (criticism) by a 30:1 ratio. Build,

build, build on strengths. Plus, your "skill" at giving negative feedback is zero on a scale of one to 10 (barely an exaggeration). Moreover, negative feedback backfires "big time;" it is research-proven Demotivator #1. (Puzzle: Why is giving regular positive feedback so difficult for so many people?)

Three-Minute Miracle #1: "I regard apologizing as the most magical, healing, restorative gesture human beings can make. It is the centerpiece of my work with executives who want to get better." / premier executive coach Marshall Goldsmith. An immediate and sincere "I'm sorry" erases virtually all sins. A three-minute, no-excuses, from-the-heart apologetic call at the right time can save a billion-dollar sale.

Standardization Sin #1: People are not "standardized." Evaluations should not be standardized. Ever. One size fits one. Iron law for leaders: every individual requires a radically different communication strategy.

Personal Habit #1: Read. Read. Then: Read. Read. Read. The most tenacious-obsessive student in any line of employment comes out on top. Age six or 66. Hall of Fame Wall Street investor: Not reading enough is "CEO shortcoming number one!"

Toughest Task #1: Numerous leadership gurus insist that effective self-management is the premier leader success attribute. And this is an unassailable fact: Your self-perception stinks. Self-management success is hour-at-a-time, bone-honest awareness and work . . . forever. And, you need lots of consistent feedback on this.

Reflection #1: "I've been thinking about the difference between the 'resume virtues' and the 'eulogy virtues.' The resume virtues are the ones you list on your resume, the skills that you bring to the job market and that contribute to external success. The eulogy virtues are deeper. They're the virtues that get talked about at your funeral, the ones that exist at the core of your being—whether you are kind, brave, honest or faithful, what kind of relationships you formed." / David Brooks. My advice, 10× today, for your and others' sakes: *Focus on the eulogy virtues!*

COVID-19 Lifelong Leadership Standard #1: Be Kind. Be Caring. Be Patient. Be Forgiving. Be Present. Be Positive. Walk in the Other Person's Shoes. "Bottom line": What you do as a leader—right now!—will be the signature of your entire career.

Afterword

Responding to Numerous Requests . . .
A Memoir

Many people have encouraged me to write a memoir. Well, finally I've given in. This book, in effect, *is* my memoir. It is solely devoted to the things I care deeply (very deeply!) about. The things that have emerged and become preoccupations ever since the day in 1966 when—fresh out of engineering school—I became a combat-engineering battalion detachment commander in Vietnam. Or the day in New York in 1977 when the Managing Director of McKinsey & Co., Ron Daniel, posed a magical question that determined my life's course: he avowed that he was sick and tired of the Firm's brilliant strategies continually failing the implementation test—what the hell was missing? Thus, though I didn't know it at the time, *In Search of Excellence* was conceived.

While researching that first book, I learned, first from Hewlett-Packard president John Young, that some leaders, the best I'd say, spent more time than one could imagine out on "the shop floor" (blue- or white-collar) getting to know and to show appreciation for the people who do the real work of the organization. This same crowd also spent "more time than one could imagine" in direct contact with customers, judging the practical and emotional impact of their products and services on the folks whose joy—or problems—make or break those leaders' companies. I spent some time observing Steve Jobs at work—and learned what a true and unyielding design obsession looks like—and the stunning results it can produce. (*In Search of Excellence* was composed on an Apple II.) I watched up close as Anita Roddick scoured the world in pursuit of partner-producers for The Body Shop who would become her suppliers and transform their communities in the process—the moral dimension of business at its best and most inspiring. Southwest Airlines founder-CEO Herb Kelleher at one point told me that, "One of my favorite jobs is penning a letter to a customer who has been abusive toward one of our employees and informing them that they are no longer welcome to fly with us." Now that's what it means to support your team members' wellbeing!

As I've said over and over in these pages—and in the pages of my first eighteen books—the ideas are not complex; they require no mastery of calculus or chemistry or physics. But the practice thereof is honored in the breach more often than not.

Collecting and sharing these ideas—Young's "Managing By Wandering Around," Kelleher's letters to misbehaving customers, Jobs' design obsession, Roddick's community-mindedness—are my life's work and, indeed, my life. They have come at the expense of millions of exhausting frequent flyer miles and a hundred, or a hundred thousand, bollixed airline connections. Yet despite horrendous messes in my travel to a destination in one of the 63 countries in which I have spoken, and I swear to this, I have never been with an audience, among the 2,500-plus that I have addressed, that I didn't deeply bond with. And, from notes I've gotten, they knew I had bonded with them—become their spiritual accompanist (and nag) on the first steps of a journey toward "people first" and, yup, Excellence. Many, if not most, subsequently fell somewhat short of my towering aspirations for them—but hundreds of letters indicated that a sizeable band had turned themselves into Kelleher or Roddick lookalikes—and discovered the emotional and "business" value of creating a turned on, growing, constantly innovating human community—numbering six or 600—of employees.

Oh Lord, I cherish especially the letters, not from CEOs, but from high school principals and fire chiefs and soccer coaches, and even an NFL coach—and, to my surprise—the occasional pastor or priest, thanking me for launching them onto a productive and joyous path. One YPO seminar attendee told me, in the presence of an audience I'd just spent eight grueling hours with, that, "I invested a day with you and learned nothing new." I guess I turned visibly pale, then listened as he continued, "But it was the best day I may ever have spent—it was a 'blinding flash of the obvious.' Take care of people, really really listen to customers, aim for no less than excellence in even the tiniest acts." I guess in the end, I am, as that participant, Manny Garcia, owner of a large chain of South Florida restaurants, implied, a BFO (Blinding Flash of the Obvious) provisioner.

Those comments are my legacy. And here in the pages of this, my nineteenth book, I share with delight and hope these ideas, these BFOs, that are my raison d'etre. Yes, this is my true and only possible memoir.

Thanks for joining me on the journey. And good luck and Godspeed!

Tom

Special Acknowledgements

Nancye Green

Stuart Lopez

Julie Anixter

Shelley Dolley

Melissa Wilson

These five made this book, this "summa," what it is.

Nancye and Stuart, in particular, offered creative suggestion after creative suggestion—far beyond the bounds of their stellar design work. (Nancye often did not make "suggestions"—she gave orders. E.g., she is responsible for the title!)

Julie Anixter is a force—the highest praise I can offer to one of my fellow human beings. She has a wonderful habit of getting ahead of all of us—her passion runneth over. And it rubs off "big time."

Shelley Dolley and I have been working partners for 20+ years. Even she admits to being *overly* meticulous; there is no detail too small for her to worry herself to near death about—to my everlasting benefit. And her premier liberal arts degree adds a flavor that no engineer-MBA (me) could ever conceive of. (How about that. Celebrate Shelley's liberal arts education and influence—and end the sentence with a dangling preposition. Sorry, Shelley.)

Melissa Wilson has done all the irreplaceable things that only a determined publisher can do. Hooray!

And:

The 30+ podcasters who asked me to talk about "Leadership in the face of Covid-19." They allowed me to figure out—one more time—how much I care about this material. Thoughtful and caring leadership in the time of Covid-19 can and should be practiced all the time. Forever and ever. Let's hope it becomes the norm.

Bob Waterman, my co-author of *In Search of Excellence*, the book that allowed me to do what I've been doing for the last several decades. Bob is all pro on ever so many dimensions— and he and his extraordinary wife, Judy, have been emotional anchors for me since 1977.

A heartfelt nod to the late Dick Anderson (Captain Richard E. Anderson USN). He was my first boss when I began my working journey as a (so-wet-behind-the-ears—I'm-soaked-just-thinking-about-it) junior combat–engineering officer in the U.S. Navy Seabees in Vietnam, age 24. Simply put, Captain Anderson is my #1 adult-life mentor. Period and unequivocally.

And, finally: Susan!!! (Were this book in color, all the exclamation marks would be bright red.)

CPSIA information can be obtained
at www.ICGtesting.com
Printed in the USA
LVHW050400060321
680700LV00010B/1342

9 781944 027940